You are not holding an ordinary book.
In your hands is a remarkable, life-transforming guide, one
that can make all the difference for you. It is deeply spiritual,
effectively practical, and saturated with heart. Delve into this
book, explore its exercises . . . and you'll reconnect with the
precious and powerful home of Spirit within you!

— Dr. Roger Teel —
AUTHOR & SPIRITUAL TEACHER

TO DAVID
WITH LOVE
AND RESPECT

Randy Pearon

THE
OPENING

EMBRACING YOUR SPIRITUAL DESTINY

RANDY FERGUSON

Published by Heart Centered Communications, Inc.
Denver, Colorado

Cover Design and Layout by MarkGelotte.com
Content Editing by Cara Cantarella and Laura High

This publication is designed to provide accurate and authoritative information in regard to the subject matter covered. The advice and strategies contained herein may not be suitable for every situation. If professional advice or other expert assistance is required, the services of a competent professional should be sought. Neither the publisher nor the author shall be held liable for damages arising from the misuse of any of the content.

For more info, visit www.LCAProject.com and www.RandyFerguson.com.
Email the author at randyf@lcaproject.com.

Library of Congress Control Number: 2018943206

Ferguson, Randy
   The Opening: Embracing Your Spiritual Destiny / Randy
Ferguson.
      xiv, 302 p., lc22.86 cm.
      ISBN: 978-0-9772758-1-6
1. Happiness, 2. Spirituality
3. Positive psychology, 4. Success,
5. Conduct of Life, 6. Self-actualization (psychology)
I. Title.   II. Ferguson, Randy

Some names and identifying details have been changed to protect the privacy of individuals.

— v. 2 . 2 —

THE

OPENING

EMBRACING YOUR SPIRITUAL DESTINY

CONTENTS

FOREWORD

I have known Randy Ferguson since I was five years old. He's my brother. At first I didn't care much for him. In fact, I didn't like him at all. Then one day I noticed something special about him. He was funny. He was witty and wise. He was actually fun to be with.

All of a sudden everything changed. It was like the sun coming out on a rainy day. We actually enjoyed being with each other. As we spent more and more time together, we became best friends. I would even take him to the grocery store to teach him how to steal candy.

I learned a lot from Randy over the years. In fact, my first introduction to enlightenment came from him. He told me that upsets never result from what happens. At the time, I thought he was crazy.

Then he explained that upsets are a state of mind and can only exist if we are fighting the truth of what happens. The quality of our lives is not the result of what happens around us. It's the result of how we relate to what happens.

This was a very profound statement and he said it in a way that I knew it was true. I couldn't argue with it. It also opened my eyes. For the first time, I understood that there is something more to life than what we see.

This started us down a path of self-discovery that would change our lives and the lives of countless others. In the years that followed, we have continued learning a great deal from life and from each other.

Randy's open heart and loving personality create an environment where people can have major healings and breakthroughs that permanently change their lives. His open heart also paved the way for something very special to happen.

He started receiving profound messages, insights and guidance from a place deep within. He seemed to have made a connection with God. He developed the ability to ask questions and actually get answers.

As he shared his discoveries, he once again changed my life. It seemed that Randy had discovered a path to something more wonderful than any of us could possibly imagine. He had discovered a path to experiencing being one with God.

In this powerful state, there is only love. We are happy, alive and free. The circumstances of life have no power. We see life clearly and have a very positive attitude. We then radiate this positive energy into life and great things happen around us.

This state is incredible, but then it gets better. As we make the connection with God, we gain a profound peace. We know deep in our heart that we are guided and taken care of. We know that God is working through us and that no matter what happens around us, our life is right on course and that we will always be okay.

This profound connection with God is available to everyone. It's like an electrical socket. Anyone can plug into it, but you need to know where it is and how to use it. That is the purpose of this book. In his beautiful, humorous and witty manner, Randy walks you through a process that will change your life as well.

— Bill Ferguson

INTRODUCTION

Consider the possibility that—

There is a presence in you, a spirit so profoundly magnificent that any words used to describe it, become instantly inadequate. This miraculous presence is the truth of who you are. It is both what you are yearning for and what you are yearning from. On the deepest level, this awesome beauty is what you have always wanted to be true. And it is in each and every one of us.

The more we come to experience this stunning inner essence, the more we passionately desire to connect with where it all comes from. We want to know the truth of our spiritual heritage. By whatever name we choose, we want to know our Maker.

Like a dandelion tenaciously piercing through asphalt, we struggle through antiquated paradigms born of a culture primitive in its wisdom. At some point, we begin to challenge these old ways of thinking and awaken to the most amazing game in the Universe—discovering the fundamentals of who we are, then living in a way that fulfills.

The purpose of this book is to validate what you know to be true and to support you in accepting life's sacred invitation. It is written in simple steps from my heart to yours.

This is your life. This is your time. The invitation is extended. You can do this! Welcome to your own grand opening.

MAXIMIZING VALUE

The most successful people I know, look for the trimtabs in life—the small things they can do that make a big difference in productivity. To get the most from this book, I'd like to offer five suggestions that will highly leverage the value you receive from your effort.

1. Most people read for knowledge or entertainment. The flow goes from author to reader. They take in the information or drama, then it's off to the next book. I'd like to offer a different possibility. As you read, imagine we're best friends, having an inspired conversation in my living room. You are my most welcomed, honored guest. This makes your experience of 'The Opening' come alive.

2. Since we are dear friends, allow your heart to come forward. Feel free to take in our conversation fully. No rush. Yes, contemplate our discussion on an intellectual level, but more importantly, feel the words as deeply as you can. In doing so, you may access internal resources you didn't know existed.

3. When I was a boy, I learned that books are sacrosanct. They are to be revered at all costs and never ever ever to be written upon. Are you willing to be a bit rebellious and throw this belief to the wind if doing so maximizes your experience? Are you willing to break the rules and write all over this text, logging-in your realizations as our adventure unfolds? At key points, I'll be asking you to write

your answers to special questions. Go ahead, keep your pen handy and write whatever you want. Be your grade school librarian's worst nightmare, enjoying yourself immensely.

4. I'll be offering "Try It Out Exercises." For so many of my seminar participants and clients, here is where they get their socks blown off. Here is where transformation occurs. In taking these action steps, you create for yourself a remarkable opportunity—to experience bringing together pieces of who you are into a whole and stunning work of art.

5. I'll also share key videos on my website (www.LCAProject.com) that go into even more detail, taking you step-by-step through the healing/growing process. In these videos we explore our topics even more deeply. Here, revelations abound as you discover what works for you in your own spiritual adventure. What difference will these videos make over time as you gather pivotal insights and personal breakthroughs that vastly increase your joy and effectiveness?

Composite Stories and Examples

Over my career, I've had the indescribable honor to work with countless seminar participants and to consult one-to-one, with over two thousand individuals. I cannot begin to express my gratitude for the insights gleaned in working together with these courageous souls. Some of my stories and examples may be a composite of these lessons learned in order to clarify a point. When referring to specific individuals, names have been changed.

DISCOVERING YOUR RELATIONSHIP WITH THAT WONDERFUL SOMETHING

Driving with my sister from the Oakland California airport, we noticed something very odd; what appeared to be a wolf standing in the middle of the highway. As we drove closer, we saw it was an elegant German Shepherd, maybe two years old. No collar or tags.

The dog lover in me was compelled to pull over. As I got out of the car, it was obvious this animal was utterly terrified.

Slowly, I walked to the side of the highway about 20 feet away from him. He looked at me as if I were the latest threat in the worst day of his life.

In that moment, something spoke to me. It said to simply love him with all my heart. So I knelt down, looked him in the eye and extended my hand. He shied back for an instant then stopped, tail tucked way beneath his legs, and glared at me.

The thought crossed my mind that I must be crazy, leaving the safety of my car. This dog could do some real damage to me if he had the inclination. Yet something told me to hold my ground, to just keep loving him intensely.

I spoke to him softly as the afternoon traffic blurred past. I told him he was going to be OK, that I would take care of him.

Afraid and confused in a crazy human world, this precious creature was being offered a life-altering invitation; an opening for something wonderful. He had a choice: to attack, to run away or to trust.

That's when it happened. To his immense credit, he chose to trust. With his head down, he took one step forward and then another. Oh so slowly he approached me, sniffed my outreached hand and surrendered.

Caressing his rich coat, I continued to reassure him. His relief was palpable. If he were human, I believe his gratitude would have been expressed in tears. I slipped my belt around his neck and led him to safety. As he lapped up the water we offered, my sister flagged down a sheriff.

The officer, obviously a fellow dog lover, promised to take special care of his new companion. Now complacent and oh so grateful, the German Shepherd leapt willingly into the back of the patrol car.

Through the rear window he just stared at me, I'm sure a bit perplexed at my leaving. Yet, even though he didn't understand the bigger picture, I knew he was in for the best chapter of his life.

And so it came to be in the midst of Oakland traffic, a frightened but courageous animal revealed one of the greatest challenges and opportunities we humans face today.

Perhaps, like the German Shepherd, you've had your share of dodging the speeding minivans of life. Perhaps you, too, are faced with a choice: to attack, to run away or to trust. And perhaps there's something inside you that is willing to take a risk—the risk required to experience an enormous shift in your quality of life.

Are you ready to savor insights, methods and encouragement

to make clear your own sacred invitation; to come to explore, love and trust a Higher Source and to claim the enormous gifts that are your spiritual destiny?

Have You Sensed It?

Can you recall reclining into lush summer grass, staring into space on a crystal clear night? Have you contemplated the notion that the twinkle from each star, originating light years apart, is now reaching your eyes at the same instant? Have you looked into the eyes of a newborn child and marveled at the magnitude of such creation? Have you experienced enough coincidences in life to know there's no way they could all be coincidental? In these special moments, have you sensed it— the presence of that Wonderful Something out there?

Is it possible there is a vastly intelligent, ridiculously powerful choreographer who organizes life in ways beyond our comprehension? If so, is it possible that you too, are a part of Its creation?

How might your life be enhanced if you discovered that you could actually live in authentic, supportive relationship with this Higher Power? What would be the impact if this partnership filled a place in your heart like nothing else ever has? And what difference would it make if you discovered with nothing less than a gut-level certainty, that you are ultimately loved, honored and cared for, regardless of circumstances?

With these questions, you are invited to embark upon what may be the most exciting, relevant and fulfilling adventure of your lifetime. Consider the possibility that the connection I'm describing offers a joy, a peace, a clarity of direction, an aliveness, a wholeness far beyond what is offered in a world of having and doing.

If you are new to your spiritual adventure, this book offers a practical pathway to the fulfillment of your yearning. If you are a seasoned seeker, you are invited to experience fresh perspectives, breath-taking vistas as we traverse new spiritual terrain. In either case, I welcome you with all my heart.

As we move forward, you'll notice I tend to refer to this Wonderful Something in the masculine, using words like, "He, Him and God." However, I've discovered that for many people, the words I use do not resonate. If my terminology doesn't work for you, please substitute words that do. "She." "Goddess." "Spirit." "Higher Power." "Universe." "Mother/ Father." "Beloved." You choose. In the words of William Shakespeare, "A rose by any other name, would smell as sweet."

What really matters is that you refer to God in a way that opens your heart to the possibility of relationship. If you were to be in authentic conversation with a loving Higher Power, what names would **you** choose?

_____

_____

_____

_____

_____

_____

_____

_____

_____

_____

_____

_____

WHAT IF—

"A rose by any other name, would smell as sweet."
– William Shakespeare

Divine Discontent

It's not that I've set any kind of radiant example when it comes to the subject of spirituality. I haven't. I've blundered my way with the best of 'em. And it's not like I know "the only way" to God. I don't. Given the people I've hurt and how I've blown it over my lifetime, who am I to tell anyone what to believe?

Yet, even a fool can say a wise thing. And it's actually in having made so many huge mistakes that I've discovered dynamics that have helped some people over the years. I am truly blessed to share a selection of these key insights with you now.

In the early nineties, I founded an organization now called the Love, Courage and Achievement Project (LCA for short). In the LCA, we take people through a transformational weekend seminar and follow-up program. In working with so many remarkable LCA participants over time, I've come to notice a fascinating trend.

There seems to be an expanding segment of our population that is ready to awaken, explore and grow. These people are ready to roll up their sleeves and do both the internal and external work required to create a dramatic shift in their quality of life.

Most of these folks have been battered a bit. They've been through divorce, layoffs, bankruptcy, deep disappointment, intense loneliness and bitter betrayal. They have come to suspect that just maybe, in their efforts to figure out life, they have been reading from the wrong instruction manual. They have followed rules for living taught in a dysfunctional culture and have painfully reaped the consequences. As a result, they are at a magical place I call "divine discontent."

Their pain is now a catalyst for change. Intuitively, they know there must be a better way to live and now they are poised for a major breakthrough.

Any chance you might be one of these folks ready to live from a different paradigm? Are you willing to step outside the box of your own mental patterns to discover a new way of being, one that truly resonates with the wisdom already living within you?

If so, let's cut to the chase and address the tough spiritual questions head on. I would ask, just for the short time we have together, that you "try on" what I'm sharing. Take what works for you and leave the rest.

Is There a God at All?

For most people, spirituality is a pretty tender issue, isn't it? More times than I can count, people I've worked with have been told what to believe and how to behave. If they didn't comply, they would be shamed and threatened with eternal damnation. So many people have been beaten over the head with religion that psychologists refer to the phenomenon as "religious abuse."

Add to the mix the incredible hypocrisy we all have witnessed by one prominent spiritual leader after another. Then add how so many good people are suffering on the planet. What does that say about how God operates, if there is a God at all?

And add to THAT, there's no way to scientifically prove the existence of God in the first place. Is it any wonder so many folks group the notion of God with Santa and the Tooth Fairy?

And yet most of us deep down, suspect there's something out there beyond our five senses. According to a recent Gallup poll, 89 percent of the U.S. population believes in some manner of Higher Power.

Redefining Reality

I received my Master's degree in Spiritual Psychology from the University of Santa Monica (USM). I loved how their curriculum was both heart-centered and keenly relevant. One of my most valuable takeaways from their program was a challenge to "redefine reality from what is provable—to what is useful."

You may have heard about two friends, a minister and a professor, who would constantly debate the existence of God. No matter how hard the minister tried to build a case for God,

WHAT IF—

You take what works for you and leave the rest.

the professor could always invalidate the evidence.

One day, the minister realized there was no way he could scientifically prove to the professor that God was real and he admitted this to his friend. Beaming in victory, the professor stood up and began to leave.

But just as he was walking out the door, the minister asked, "By the way, how are your kids?"

The professor beamed again and said, "Oh they're doing great."

The minister then asked something strange. He inquired, "Do you love them?"

The professor was a bit offended by the question. He said, "Well, of course I love them."

At which point the minister paused, then said softly, "Prove it."

This story drives home a point: things exist in this Universe that are priceless in value, yet do not lend themselves to quantification—things like caring—like love—like God. Does that resonate as true for you?

Could it be to your benefit as well, to redefine reality from what is provable to what is useful? Could being in loving partnership with an all-knowing, all-powerful, all-present, all-available beingness—be of value even if you can't quantify its existence?

I love this saying, "To the mind, there is never enough evidence to prove the existence of God. And to the heart, none is required."

WHAT IF—

*It could be to your benefit as well, to redefine reality
from what is provable to what is useful.*

WHAT IF—

*To the mind, there is never enough evidence
to prove the existence of God.
To the heart, none is required.*

Of course this redefining of reality does not preclude the usefulness of what is provable. Logic has its place. I am so grateful for science, for western medicine and the conveniences of technology in its many forms.

Nor am I saying "if it feels good, do it." Sometimes doing the right thing doesn't feel good at all. Right action can be extremely difficult and downright painful.

What I am suggesting is that in expanding our definition of reality, we can come to know priceless dimensions of existence that would otherwise go unexplored. If you are willing to embrace this new definition of reality, doors of possibility begin to appear that were otherwise impossible to see. You begin to notice new truths that once identified, can change your life forever.

There's No Going Back

There once was a native who lived deep in the jungle. One day, this man and his family came upon an automobile, something they had never seen nor heard of before. He sat in the driver's seat, fascinated by the rear view mirror. When his family members began pushing the car forward, he grabbed on to the mirror and twisted it to the right. By coincidence, the car turned to the right. Then he twisted the mirror to the left but the car turned even more to the right and ran into a tree.

Just then another native showed up who had been to the city before. She explained how to use something called a steering wheel. From that point forward, do you think he ever again tried turning the car with the rear view mirror? No way!

In the same manner, when people hear laws and dynamics that resonate in their hearts, they acquire a knowing they hadn't put together before, and can never quite go back to the way it was.

So, you may want to try a few of these "steering wheel" ideas, on for size as we continue to explore the question, "Who or what is God?"

Who (or What) is God?

I was raised in the Christian faith. As a family, we would go to church, pray before meals and read Bible stories before we slept. At summer camp, I had an experience of consciously surrendering my life to Jesus and that relationship has only grown more beautiful over the years. In fact, it's grown beyond the confines of traditional religion to the point where now I call myself a renegade Christian. Allow me to explain.

When I was a senior at Arizona State, I recall going through some real spiritual turmoil. I didn't doubt the existence of God, but I was very confused about how it all worked in the real world. What should I believe? Are biblical scriptures to be taken literally? Where is this inquiry going to take me? Am I going to end up as some kind of religious fanatic screaming "Praise the Lord" on a street corner?

To find answers to these questions, I went on a quest, exploring an array of religious organizations. As a result, I became even more confused and frustrated.

Why? Because every organization I visited had two things in common: 1) Each one knew they had THE answer, and 2) Every organization's answer was different.

How could this be? Who had the truth? Who should I believe? This inner turmoil went on for quite a while.

It's funny where we get our answers sometimes. I happened upon the work of a Danish poet by the name of Piet Hein. Here's the little poem that gave me the answer I was seeking:

I am a humble artist
Molding my earthly clod.
Adding my lot to nature's,
simply assisting God.

Not that my effort is needed,
yet somehow, I understand
God willed it, I too should have,
unmolded clay in my hand.

This simple poem moved me and revealed that the answers I sought, weren't going to come from deciding which religious leader to follow. The answers I yearned for would come by molding my own clay; looking inside, listening to and trusting the resonance in my own heart. From that point forward, that's what I did. I chose not to embrace a spiritual belief unless it resonated within. And all these years later, I've never regretted that decision.

Trusting Your Inner Wisdom

Could this realization be useful for you in your spiritual journey? Consider this. Have you ever experienced an "ah ha?" Perhaps you were having a conversation with a friend, reading a book, watching a movie—when suddenly, you became clear on something you didn't understand before.

Well, how could you have experienced that "ah ha" if it didn't resonate with a body of wisdom already living within you? Just like two identical tuning forks, both of which resonate when you strike just one—is it possible that truth resonates with a reservoir of wisdom you already have deep within?

Look in your own life. Don't you also have a remarkable ability to discern when a truth is spoken? And don't you also know

WHAT IF—

You have experienced "ah ha's" because the truth resonates with a reservoir of wisdom that is already within you.

when something doesn't sound or feel quite right? So, as we proceed, are you willing to listen to your own knowing that already lives within?

As I ask you to consider different possibilities, look inside your own reservoir of wisdom to see if they resonate for you. Wrestle with them a bit. Explore within yourself. If these insights add value, keep them for your own. And as I said, if they don't, just let them go. Would that be OK with you?

What's Love Got to Do With It?

Consider the possibility that God is not a punishing, bearded old man in the sky, racking up points against you, poised to cast you into some eternal furnace. Consider the possibility that God is love itself; as I shared, an all-knowing, all-powerful, all-present, all-loving, all-available being-ness.

I'm not going to quote volumes of Biblical scripture in the pages to come, but this particular line says it well: "Whoever does not love, does not know God, because God is love." 1 John 4:8

Yet, how could that be, given all the intense suffering on the planet? How could an all-powerful, all-loving God allow such horrendous travesties?

Consider the possibility there is a fairly sizable gap between humanity's intellectual/technological prowess and humanity's emotional maturity. In other words, we can unravel the DNA code, send missions to Mars, and video conference via satellite from anywhere on the planet. But just try keeping a family together, or maintaining peak self-esteem for more than a few days, or overcoming long term destructive habits. In other words, humankind has some room for inner improvement.

Consider also, the possibility that life is a school. The purpose of this school is to bring us the life lessons required to grow us in our wisdom, so we can close this gap, becoming the very best versions of ourselves.

Humankind, however, hasn't been as interested in learning these lessons as we've been interested in making ourselves comfortable in the world. Another way of saying this is that for the most part, we have been committed to our comfort whether or not it's fulfilling. In contrast, God is committed to our fulfilment whether or not it's comfortable. Hmmmm.

Here's Something We Call the LCA Wisdom Curve

On the horizontal axis, we have something called Time and on the vertical axis we have something called Wisdom (which as you know is very different from intelligence). Consider the possibility that as we proceed over time, we are continually invited by God to grow up the Wisdom Curve.

As part of our divine curriculum, we are brought just the right lessons required to grow us, and we are brought these lessons whether we like it or not. Does this ring true for you?

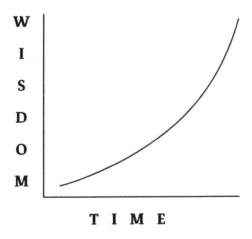

Every day we are invited to evolve into a more effective, kinder, wiser, more joyful, God-like person while we are here on earth in human form.

So, if that's the game plan, do we have to go along with it? Absolutely not. We have free will and get to make choices whether those choices are constructive or destructive. We can live congruently or incongruently with the laws of the Universe. When we live in alignment with how life works, we thrive. When we live contrary to how life works, we suffer. But in either case, it's our choice.

In the words of Cecil B DeMille, "It is impossible for us to break the law. We can only break ourselves against the law." In other words, God allows us to run full speed into a brick wall over and over again if that's what we choose to do. But just down the road a piece is something called a door that makes passing through walls much easier. Our job is to grow in our wisdom so we can find more doors.

Love Lessons

Consider the possibility that out of our lack of wisdom, we are the ones who have made a pretty good mess of things on Earth. Individually, we have created things like divorce, resentment, addiction, bankruptcy and estrangement. Collectively, we have created war, prejudice, tyranny, poverty, mass starvation and genocide.

So, just maybe, God isn't making bad things happen, nor is He doling out punishment. He's bringing us the lessons we need so we can grow in our wisdom and learn how to love. And this is true for us both as individuals and as nations.

My brother, Bill Ferguson, who also does this work, once said something that shook me to the core.

WHAT IF—

We have been committed to our comfort
whether or not it's fulfilling.
God is committed to our fulfilment whether
or not it's comfortable.

WHAT IF—

God isn't making bad things happen,
nor is He doling out punishment.
He's bringing us the lessons we need so we can
grow in our wisdom and learn how to love.

He said, "You know, the world doesn't need changing."

I said, "What? Are you nuts? Don't you listen to the news? What do you mean—the world doesn't need changing?" (Brothers can talk to each other this way.)

He looked right at me and said, "It's true. The world doesn't need changing. If you could push a button and instantly there would be no suffering, no war, no tyranny, no disease, no crime, no terrorism—if all the atrocities were removed, and there wasn't love—in a matter of days, things would go right back to the way that they were."

He said, "What the world needs most is to learn how to love. Only then will change be significant and lasting."

(I just love that guy).

So what or who is God? Consider the possibility that God is not the one causing such suffering on the planet. Consider the possibility that God is the one teaching us to love so needless suffering can become a thing of the past.

Is It Really Possible to Connect With God—One on One?

If there really is a God and the nature of God is Love, isn't it only natural that we would yearn for authentic connection; to be in genuine heart-centered communication?

Consider the possibility that if our hearts are open, we can literally live in relationship and partnership with God. We can actually be in communication with Him, ask questions and receive some pretty remarkable answers. The purpose of the rest of this book is to share a pathway to making this connection real.

For several years now, I have been keeping a God Journal.

WHAT IF—

*"The world doesn't need changing.
What the world needs most is to learn how to love.
Only then will change be significant and lasting."*
— Bill Ferguson

WHAT IF—

*God is not the one causing such suffering
on the planet. Consider the possibility that God is
the one teaching us to love so needless suffering
can become a thing of the past.*

I wish God "Good Morning" and he returns the greeting. I ask him questions and He answers with wisdom far senior to my own. I believe most anybody can do this with a little guidance and practice.

A while back, God offered what has become nothing less than a spiritual toolbox to assist me in my journey. These tools have become the foundation for my life. They are the bedrock upon which I live, and I contemplate them most every day. He says they are the key to living our highest and greatest potential—to attaining true fulfilment—to ascending as high as we can as human beings in our lifetime. He refers to these tools as the "Sacred Six," a paradigm for living radically different from how most people operate. I share them with you now from my heart to yours, to do with as you wish.

THE SACRED SIX

6 INVITATIONS FOR HUMAN FULFILLMENT

#1 - LOVE GOD WITH ALL YOUR HEART, SOUL, MIND AND STRENGTH

(This may sound familiar to some of you)

What Happens When You Love?

Let's do a little exercise. Just for a moment, recall a time when you were in the presence of someone who truly loved you with all their heart; not a clingy kind of love, but a pure, beautiful, unconditional love. Now close your eyes, take a deep breath and allow yourself, just for a moment, to be immersed in this experience.

Next, write your answers to these two questions:

Who was the person who loved you in this way?

_____

When you were in this experience of love, what else were you feeling? What else was present for you?

_____
_____
_____
_____
_____

When I offer this inquiry in seminars, participants share how they feel a deep peace, joy, aliveness and unconditional acceptance. Their fear, resentment and attachment fall away and in that moment they experience a sense of belonging, clarity, safety, wholeness, a flow of creativity and oneness; a cornucopia of life's most meaningful gifts. To the extent we experience love, life is great. To the extent it is absent, we live with a deadness, an emptiness inside. Isn't this true regardless of what we have parked in the garage or the numbers on our bank statement?

Consider the possibility that God wants you to love so that you'll have these priceless gifts. He asks you to love Him, not because He needs it or because you should. He commands us to love Him because it works.

What Really Determines Quality of Life?

Notice also the role love plays in determining our very quality of life. In our culture, we are taught that quality of life is directly related to standard of living. We believe that the more our circumstances are accumulated and arranged in just the right way, the happier we'll be. The formula we're taught looks like this:

Quality of Life is determined by — Standard of Living

The advertising industry thrives on this assumption. Buy our deodorant and the man of your dreams will sweep you away into a world of bliss. Purchase our insurance and you will be insulated from worry forever. Basically, buy our service or product, and you will be happy.

However, when we test this theory, it falls apart. Can you absolutely count on your standard of living to determine your quality of life? Have you ever had your circumstances arranged in a way others would envy, but experienced an internal void? Or have you ever been in a place financially where you didn't know where your next dollar was coming from, yet felt a sense of joy and contentment inside?

I recall a time in my twenties when I first began making some money in real estate. I had restored a 1959 XK-150 Jaguar convertible. It had big rounded fenders, high gloss grey lacquer paint, red leather upholstery, a luggage rack, and polished chrome spinners on red spoked wheels. It was the perfect mate magnet.

One day I was touring the Jag through downtown Denver. As usual, other drivers were staring at me with admiration. Yet in that particular moment I recall feeling utterly empty inside. I realized they had no idea who the driver was, and at that time, neither did I. That's when I began to discover that I cannot count on standard of living to determine quality of life.

Don't get me wrong—I appreciate the physical goodies in life as much as the next guy. It's just that I know I can't count on material wealth to deliver what matters most.

Yet, there is something I can count on 100 percent of the time, 24/7, to determine quality of life. When I am in the experience of love, my quality of life is always, always, always in a peak state. Is this true for you as well? If so, perhaps a more useful formula looks like this:

Quality of Life is determined by — The Experience of Loving

Could this simple realization be an essential ingredient to what we have been seeking? If so, as a practical matter, how do we do this? How do we go about creating this experience of love in the real world?

There are two alternatives. First, you can wait for people and circumstances to behave in just the right way, so you will feel loved. Of course, this option gives all your power to create love to the people and circumstances around you and could result in a rather long wait.

The second option is to take the initiative to create love around you. What would it be like if you could create the experience of love (thereby ramping up your own quality of life) as easily as turning on a light switch? How cool would that be?

You absolutely have the power and ability to do this. Here's the key. What it takes to have love, is to give love. How? By deliberately offering the gift of unconditional acceptance and deep appreciation. The more you put it out there, the more you tend to get it back.

And in the instant you experience love for another, you too are enveloped in the gift. The moment you give love, you're in love.

Why Love God?

So what happens when you unconditionally accept and deeply appreciate God? Something magical.

With anything you love, you create relationship. This is true with your spouse, your kids, your pets, your new briefcase, your lawn mower—anything. Whenever you love, you create connection. When you love God, you create a relationship with an all-knowing, all-powerful, all-present, all-loving, all-available being-ness. Not a bad partner to have.

Also, when you love God, your heart opens to seeing that you are loved BY God. The more you love Him, the more you

WHAT IF—

What creates the experience of love, is giving the gift of unconditional acceptance and deep appreciation.

WHAT IF—

The moment you give love, you're in love.

WHAT IF—

With anything you love, you create relationship.

feel loved by Him. The more you feel loved by the Creator of the Universe, the more precious you feel, regardless of the circumstances.When you feel loved by God, you become open to receiving extraordinary good. This becomes a very powerful upward cycle. And one really magnificent thing about God is His dependability. Where people can become upset, lash out, betray and abandon—God will not. He is with you for the duration.

Herein lies a profound possibility—the creation of an awesome, 100 percent dependable relationship with God—a friendship, a union, a oneness that changes everything. The instant you experience this union, your life will never be the same.

How do you go about this? To create a relationship with God, ask for a relationship with God. Just ask Him. Pray. Whatever words you use will be perfect. It doesn't have to be eloquent. You don't have to do it right. Just ask Him with all your heart and watch what happens. Would you like to take a brief break here (only if you're ready) and just ask Him?

Open your heart. Be patient. Give up the need to control and to understand. You will never understand God, because God does not live in the realm of understanding. He lives in the realm of your heart.

When you love God, you open yourself to a different kind of knowing. It's not an intellectually based kind of understanding, but rather a deep, heart-centered wisdom.

A teacher once asked his student to walk over to a homeless man and to love him. The student replied, "How can I possibly love that man if I don't even know him?"

The teacher responded, "How can you possibly know the man if you don't love him?"

WHAT IF—

The more you feel loved by the Creator of the Universe, the more precious you feel, regardless of the circumstances. When you're loved by God, you become open to receiving extraordinary good. This becomes a very powerful upward cycle.

WHAT IF—

Where people can become upset, lash out, betray and abandon—God will not. He is with you for the duration.

Try It Out Exercise: Feel the Presence of God

Step 1:

Claim twenty minutes of your day just for you with no inter-ruptions. Hang a "Do Not Disturb" sign on your door if you must. This is your time. Light a candle and ask with all your heart to experience the loving presence and assistance of God in this exercise, feeling grateful for knowing your prayer is already answered.

Sit or kneel in a comfortable position. You may wish to watch the video titled, "Feel the Presence of God" so I can guide you through the steps:

www.lcaproject.com/the-opening-videos

Step 2:

Now close your eyes just for a few moments as you breathe deeply. Imagine yourself in the center of a beautiful white and gold column of light—the light of love itself, the Light of God. To the best of your ability, experience this light slowly turning, surrounding you with its infinite loving and healing. Imagine this beautiful light especially focused into the area of your physical heart. Now experience this light of love expanding, permeating your body, bringing vibrant joy and health to everything it illuminates. Feel your body absorbing its stunningly beautiful brilliance and warmth.

As this stunning white and gold column of light continues to swirl and turn within you, notice how it slowly continues to grow, now filling your entire chest, then your neck and head. Swirling and churning, everything it shines upon joins in this symphony of profound joy, radiant health and vibrant aliveness.

The light continues to expand, filling your shoulders, radiating down through your arms, wrists and hands. Now it continues down through your abdomen your hips, buttocks, upper and lower legs, into your feet.

Feel your entire body utterly filled with this sacred light of love. Feel a sense of being fully alive, a joyful sense of gratitude infinitely more powerful than anything you've ever experienced.

Now, in this place of total fulfilment, imagine yourself walking through a forest of indescribable beauty. You are surrounded by the most beautiful plants and flowers you've ever seen. Never before have you experienced colors this intense. The fragrances are beyond anything you've ever smelled. As you drink in the nectar of this moment, notice that you are totally fulfilled. Truly, there's no other place you would rather be.

Treasuring each step, you look up and notice someone in the distance, another being of light. As you approach this being, you feel your heart soar even higher. You are in a state of awe, humbled to be in the presence of such wisdom, such power, such loving. Looking into the eyes of this being is an experience like coming home.

With indescribable loving, this being of Light reaches out and oh so gently caresses your cheek. And in an instant, you know something deep within you has awakened.

In this divine moment, you are invited to ask anything you wish. If you want this level of ecstasy in your life, you simply need to ask. If you want an ongoing relationship with God, you simply need to ask. What is the desire of your heart?

Take a moment now and ask any question you desire. Then listen.

Is there anything this sacred being has to share with you?

Very good. Now, is there anything else you wish to ask in this space of profound connection? Again, just ask and listen.

Thank you. When you're ready, just say goodbye for now, knowing you may return to this sacred space any time you choose to do so.

Remaining in this state of utter contentment, begin to bring yourself back into the physical realm. Feel your physical surroundings and prepare to come back into the room. When you're ready, come on back. Take a deep breath and allow your eyes to open.

Great. Welcome back.

Step 3:

Now, if you want, just journal here a bit. What was this experience like for you? What communications did you receive?

_____
_____
_____
_____
_____
_____
_____
_____
_____
_____
_____
_____
_____
_____
_____

What might be the benefits of opening your heart to living in relationship with a God beyond your understanding?

_____
_____
_____
_____
_____
_____
_____
_____
_____
_____
_____
_____

What would change in your life if you made this connection on a regular basis?

_____
_____
_____
_____
_____
_____
_____
_____
_____
_____
_____
_____

Step 4:

Take a moment and just say thank you for the way your prayer was answered.

THE SACRED SIX:

#2 - LOVE YOURSELF AND OTHERS WITH ALL YOUR HEART, SOUL, MIND AND STRENGTH

In those quiet moments, years ago, God offered me a second instruction that perplexed me at first. He said to "Love yourself and others with all your heart, soul mind and strength" and He said to do so in that order—first to love self, then to love others.

This sounded a bit selfish to me. Egotistical. But then I came to understand that I am the single human being on the planet with whom I spend the most time. I realized that just as I have a relationship with God, I actually have a relationship with Randy, and the quality of this relationship affects every aspect of my life, especially my relationships with others.

In our culture, we're taught you have a relationship with friends, family members and co-workers. But we're not taught that you have a relationship with self. And yet we do.

If you take a look, isn't there a way that you speak to you, a way that you treat you, and a way that you regard you? When people first realize this, their very next words are often, "Yes, and that relationship could use some work!"

I ask audiences, "How many of you are harder on yourself than you are with anyone else?" Most every hand goes up.

Your Relationship With You

So what is the quality of your relationship with you?

Imagine for a moment a beautiful mansion. As you enter, you notice a majestic staircase leading up to a gorgeous balcony with marble floors. In the center of this balcony is a small table with an exquisite linen tablecloth. On this tablecloth is a large antique porcelain vase with fresh-cut willow branches. This vase is an heirloom entrusted from mother to mother for generations.

As you watch from a distance, a tiny child walks up to the table. This little one has watched mom change tablecloths and now it is time to change this one. As the child pulls the fabric, the vase moves, then begins to teeter on the table's edge.

Just then, mom turns the corner and sees what's happening. She lunges forward trying to save the vase, but it's too late. It slams onto that marble floor, exploding into a million pieces as the child stares in wide-eyed shock.

The question then becomes, how should mom handle this situation? Of course we all know the answer.

Mom picks up one of the larger willow branches and begins to strike the child. As hard as she can, she whips those tiny hands and arms. And every time the child tries to stand, she delivers more and more welts on those now-bleeding little legs and back. She does this over and over and over, until eventually, the child cannot move at all.

Does this story bother you? Is there a part of you that cries out with indignation, "No! Why are you writing this? This isn't right! Stop it!"

WHAT IF—

*What is the quality of your relationship
with you ?*

I couldn't agree more. Which brings up the question: Is the little child within you any less precious than the little child in this story? Consider the possibility—might now be a good time for you to lay down the willows?

Or should the beatings continue?

Judging and condemning your self is like punching holes in a boat to make it go faster—somewhat less than effective. In this work, we have a saying: "You will never ever, ever, ever, ever, beat yourself into magnificence." This is because the more we judge ourselves, the more we decimate our self-esteem and the less capable in life we become.

In the Sacred Six, you are asked to do the exact opposite. You are asked to unconditionally accept and deeply appreciate who you are, the way you are right now. This is not abdicating your responsibility to improve. It's simply embracing the precious-ness of who you are right now—because in this moment, aren't you exactly the way you are? And aren't you exactly the way you are, whether you like it or not? Are you willing to love this amazing creation called "you"—even if you have room for improvement—even if you've made mistakes in the past?

Who's going to be more powerful in creating constructive change in our world, someone who beats self to a pulp or someone with true self esteem?

What Would Change if You Truly Loved You?

Just imagine, what difference would it make if you experienced a genuine love for yourself on a consistent basis? Yet for many people, there is a reluctance to do this. The fear is that if we really stoked the furnace of our self-regard, others would judge us as conceited and arrogant. Well, is there a difference between confidence and arrogance? Have you

WHAT IF—

*Is now a good time for you to lay down the willows?
Or should the beatings continue?*

WHAT IF—

*You will never ever, ever, ever, ever, beat yourself
into magnificence.*

WHAT IF—

*Who is going to be more powerful in creating
constructive change in our world, someone who
beats self to a pulp or someone with
true self esteem?*

ever known someone who was very confident but also had a genuinely humble spirit?

So, here's the question. Are you willing to give the gift of unconditional acceptance and deep appreciation to your precious self with all your heart, soul, mind and strength? Are you willing to love yourself as intensely as you have ever loved anyone on the planet?

What might you achieve in life if you didn't fight against yourself? What difference could you make if you gave yourself the gift of unconditional acceptance and deep appreciation? Are you willing to receive and give a gift of this enormity? If you are willing, the next question for many is "How?" How do you actually go about loving your precious self?

A key to success seems to be in deliberately managing our inner conversations and outer actions in ways that reflect self-caring. At the end of this chapter I'll share an empowerment exercise that is very effective in accomplishing this vital shift.

One of my individual consulting clients came to me for his last session quite upset. He said, "Randy, over the last couple months, I've had such magnificent breakthroughs. I've felt so much peace, so close to God. But this last week I lost it all. I'm out of the Light and can't understand why! What happened?!"

He was really in a place of hurting.

I shared with him that living the Sacred Six isn't always about feeling good. He discovered that what creates the experience of love isn't trying to feel a certain way. It's far more about embracing the way you feel right now, however that may be. That's what love does—it embraces things the way they are.

He looked at me in that strange way people do when they're

having a breakthrough and said, "You mean I don't HAVE to be happy all the time? What a relief! Thank God!!!" Then he got this enormous grin on his face. We both couldn't help but break out laughing.

I asked God once why I don't seem to be able to live in the experience of love all the time and His answer was so very useful. He said, "Randy, you are not yet in a place where you can feel My presence constantly, but you are getting closer.

For now, know that when you do not feel Me near, you are being invited to grow. This is as it should be, beautiful and perfect. Remember, at any given moment you are either home or you have a place to return home to."

God is love and love says, "I know you. I know everything about you. Everything. I know what you call your absolute awfulness and your most compelling beauty." Love says, "I created you with a soul, free will and fallibility. And I did a great job!"

Loving One Another

Now, are you willing to expand this gift of loving to the people around you? Notice what it's like to be around someone who truly sees, accepts and values you. Don't you respond to them in a special way?

As I shared, the more you give love, the more love tends to be returned. There's no way you can love someone and not be immersed in the experience yourself. So the more we create the experience of love, the more we generate a spiritual environment that seems to feed our very soul. And this we can do consciously. Deliberately. Moment by moment. In the LCA, we have a bumper magnet that says "Don't fall in love—Jump!" If you want one, go to: www.lcaproject.com/shop.

Of course, we've offered our loving in the past and things have not always gone as planned. Have you ever extended your heart to someone you loved and trusted, only to have it kicked through the goal posts of life? What did you decide in that instant about extending your heart again? Do the words "I will never, ever, ever let myself get hurt like that again!" sound familiar?

Most people, in an act of protection, begin building the "walls" after an experience like that. In order to avoid being hurt again, we have hardened our hearts and in so doing, have actually pushed away what we want more than anything in the world—true intimacy—the experience of loving and of being loved.

We decide that love itself is the enemy, that we can live just fine without it. And we can. We can go years without feeling love. But this ultimately culminates in a life of diversions, a life of just getting by, a life devoid of true joy. And that's just not what we are designed for, is it?

So perhaps the real culprit here isn't love. It's not knowing how to deal with hurt and not knowing how to forgive.

How to Deal With Hurt

It had been three years since Emily discovered her husband was having an affair with her best friend. She came to me to do something about the intense bitterness she continued to harbor inside. There was a hardness in her words and mannerisms. Her ongoing resentment manifested in recurring loneliness, depression, stress and ulcers.

I asked her about the messages she had been given as a child regarding experiencing hurt. She said her mom would tell her to "just get over it." Dad said, "You want to cry? I'll give you

WHAT IF—

*"At any given moment you are either home
or you have a place to return home to."*
—God

WHAT IF—

Don't fall in love—Jump!

WHAT IF—

*The culprit is not knowing how to deal with hurt
and not knowing how to forgive.*

something to cry about." At a certain age on the playground, to shed a tear meant absolute and relentless ridicule.

As a result, Emily learned in no uncertain terms, that it was NOT OK to experience her hurt when she was hurt. She learned to tough it out, to stuff it down deep inside and go on with life.

That's when I shared with her the two distinct yet opposite ways to relate to hurt. One way keeps hurt stuck for decades. The other way allows us to clear hurt in minutes.

In the first option, she discovered the more she avoided feeling hurt, the more her hurt remained and festered. What she resisted, persisted. The tougher she got, the tougher life was for her. She saw this option is by far the least effective and the one most prevalently demonstrated in our culture.

In the second option, I challenged her to redefine the word, "courage." I shared with her that just about anyone can stuff the hurt and build the walls. Real courage shows up in one's willingness to face the hurt head-on and experience it fully, to let it come and to let it go, just like a little child.

Emily saw the value in the second option, but was reluctant to go after her hurt and feel it fully. Her fear was that if she opened up the reservoir of her tears, she would cry forever. But then she realized that the more she was willing to feel her pain, the quicker it would heal. Finally, she said, "OK. Option one sure hasn't been working. I'm willing for the second alternative."

Of course, without her willingness, we could go no further because she was the one in charge. But with her willingness, the door was now open for something wonderful to happen.

WHAT IF—

*Just about anyone can stuff the hurt
and build the walls. Real courage shows up
in one's willingness to face the hurt head-on
and experience it fully, to let it come and to let it go,
just like a little child.*

How to Forgive

Consider the possibility that the experience of love and the experience of resentment are mutually exclusive. Until we forgive, we cannot fully love ourselves or another.

So to get the very most from Emily's continuing story, please allow me to ask you a few questions. In this way you can heal any resentment you may have right along with her.

What happens when we are in the experience of love, and then recall someone we have been resenting? Doesn't that feeling of love fly out the window?

When you are truly honest with yourself, for whom do you hold the most resentment?

_____

_____

What has hanging on to this resentment cost you?

_____

_____

Are you willing to allow your hurt to come up—to feel the sadness fully just like Emily—if that's what it takes to be free inside?

_____

Emily began to realize that forgiveness is not a statement that another's hurtful behavior was OK. What they did WASN'T OK. Forgiveness is about releasing toxic bitterness within one's self. As she became even more clear about what her resentment had been costing her (the anger, the anxiety, the

WHAT IF—

The experience of love and the experience of resentment are mutually exclusive. Until we forgive, we cannot fully love ourselves or another.

sabotaged relationships, the physical suffering, the loss of enjoyment.) she became even more determined to get to the other side.

I asked Emily to tell me of a time when she personally, had made a mistake that really hurt someone. She told me of an incident in middle school when she was 13 and really wanted to be popular. Her best friend since kindergarten was considered to be somewhat geeky in the minds of the more popular girls, so Emily broke off her long-term friendship with unkind words. Of course her friend was hurt deeply and eventually went on her way. Emily never made amends and had carried that guilt for decades.

Can you recall a time when you did something that hurt someone in the past? Who did you hurt?

_____

And what did you do that hurt them?

_____

_____

_____

_____

I thanked her for being so honest and asked her to consider the notion that every person has a reality from which they see life. This reality is like the operating system of a computer. Without it, a computer cannot function and neither can we.

I also shared that we take action from this reality and this is true regardless of where we are on the Wisdom Curve. For example, when we were five years old, we had the reality of a five-year-old. From that reality, we acted the way five-year-olds act. There's no way we could do otherwise. Wherever we are on the Wisdom Curve, we have a way of seeing life and behave accordingly.

So here's how it looks:

Emily looked back in time and recalled what she did that hurt her little friend in middle school. She exclaimed how awful her action was and that she should have known better. What she didn't notice was that she was looking back from the wisdom of a 45 year-old.

The truth, however, is that at age 13, Emily DIDN'T know better! At least, she didn't know better enough to alter her actions. Why? Because at that point, she only had the wisdom of a 13 year-old.

So the lie that keeps resentment stuck is that the person should have been wiser than they were, which of course is impossible. This insight makes forgiveness viable.

In fact, it took a lesson like this to teach Emily the consequences of hurting another and the value in loyalty—wisdom that was essential in the years to come.

In the dialogue that follows, I invite you to engage in a way that is meaningful in your own healing. Line by line, you might consider noticing how Emily's story applies to you.

Randy: Emily, would you like to heal this resentment you have been holding against your former husband and best friend?

Emily: Yes. It's time to let it go.

Randy: Good. Emily, at age 13, do you see that you had a particular way of seeing life—a reality from which you saw the world?

Emily: Yes.

Randy: Do you see that you were operating consistently with that reality at age 13, when you hurt her best friend?

Emily: (Beginning to tear) Yes, but I should have known better. What I did was really cruel!

Randy: That's right, what you did was cruel. And if you could take today's reality as a 45 year-old, back in time, would you have handled things differently?

Emily: (Emphatically) Yes, of course! But I can't really do that can I?

Randy: No, you can't. The best you can do is to learn and forgive; to get deeply that, given your very limited reality at age 13, you COULDN'T have done it differently. What you knew to do back then was to end your friendship so you could be more popular, and that's what you did.

Emily: But I knew it was wrong, even as I did it!

(Tears streaming now)

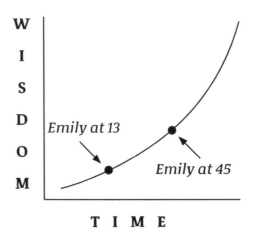

WHAT IF—

*The lie that keeps resentment stuck is that the person
should have been wiser than they were,
which of course is impossible.
This insight makes forgiveness viable.*

Randy: Yes, that's true. But you didn't know it enough to change your behavior, did you?

Emily: No, I guess not.

Randy: So the question is, are you willing to forgive Emily for having the reality of a 13 year-old, given that she COULDN'T have done it any differently?

Emily: (After taking a moment to work it inside, Emily nods her head.) Yes.

Randy: So are you willing to forgive Emily for not being wiser and more aware?

Emily: (She looks up) Yes. I'm willing.

Randy: Thank you. Emily, would you be willing to do a little visualization exercise with me?

Emily: OK. Yes.

Randy: Close your eyes and imagine yourself as you are today, going back in time. Imagine walking up to that 13 year-old Emily right after she had hurt her childhood friend."

Imagine that the younger Emily is feeling absolutely awful. She looks up and recognizes you as an older version of herself, someone who loves her completely.

Now see that 13 year-old running up to you, throwing her arms around you and saying, "Oh, I'm so sorry. What was I thinking? And she weeps in your arms. Imagine just holding this young girl as she cries and cries and cries.

(When her tears begin to subside) What is it you would like to say to say to this 13 year-old Emily?

Emily: (Softly with arms wrapped around herself.) It's OK, baby. You made a mistake just like we all do. You learned something important. It's going to be OK. I'm right here for you.

(Emily takes this in, then opens her eyes, and comes present)

Randy: So do you forgive that 13 year-old even though she made a big mistake?

Emily: Yes. I do forgive her. She couldn't have done it any differently from where she was.

Randy: How does that feel inside"

Emily: Lighter. Much lighter.

Randy: Very good. Now recall your former husband and your best friend of later years. Do you see that they, too, had their place on the wisdom curve when they betrayed you?

And just like you, do you see that they made decisions from a very limited place on the Wisdom Curve?

After years of fighting the agony of this double betrayal, Emily let the dam (or damn) of emotion break open. She cried full out. Her body shook—heaving sobs about losing the two people she loved the most in the world. She cried and cried and cried. Then she came to the end of her tears and for the first time in years, began to feel some peace.

Are you willing to release the dam of your own emotion?

Are you willing to let it go now?

_____

_____

Randy: Emily, are you willing to forgive your ex-husband and your best friend for not being wiser and more aware?

Emily: Yes, I am. I do. They did the best they could with what they had.

Those two creeps!
(Laughter)

Now Emily could forgive the unforgiveable and move on with her life. The loneliness, depression, stress and ulcers subsided, but that wasn't the best part. There were enormous gifts yet to unfold in this life lesson.

Emily embraced her learning and grew up the Wisdom Curve in a big way. She now had the means to release her hurt and live free of resentment which cleared the way for more love than she'd ever experienced.

From this point forward, whenever Emily got hurt, she could release her suffering just like her own children did so naturally. She realized pain is hurt resisted—healing is hurt embraced. And ironically, the more she was willing to experience her hurt, the less fear she had of its happening again. This realization was a game changer! Now she could take the intelligent risks that would bring forward her dreams.

These breakthroughs allowed her to love fully once again, which was by far the greatest gift of all. Now she could drop her walls and risk extending love, full out. She could love unconditionally with all her heart.

Little did she know she was doing the very inner work required to attract a very special partner. Not long afterwards, she fell in love and married a remarkable man who became both a great husband and stepfather.

WHAT IF—

Pain is hurt resisted. Healing is hurt embraced.

WHAT IF—

*The more you are willing to experience your hurt,
the less fear you have of its happening again.
This realization is a game changer!*

Years later, she made a fascinating comment. She said, "Had I not been betrayed, I would not have learned the lessons required for the best years of my life. Now I'm the one who initiates love without the condition that others return it. You would not believe how much love comes back to me!"

Were you able to garner some of the benefits of Emily's journey? What are you discovering about forgiveness and how do you feel?

_____
_____
_____
_____
_____
_____
_____
_____
_____
_____
_____
_____

What is Empowerment?

Empowerment is love communicated. It is the ability to share what you appreciate in yourself or another specifically, authentically and from your heart. It is possible to consciously create the experience of love for yourself and others with everything you've got—to see the magnificence that we are as human beings and express it.

Empower yourself, your spouse, your friends, your family and co-workers. Empower the cashier at the grocery store. Become an empowerment machine. Then notice what happens to

WHAT IF—

Empowerment is love communicated.
It is the ability to share what you appreciate
in another specifically, authentically and
from your heart.

your quality of life as more and more love is reflected back to you on a daily basis.

Love for many of us is like the flame in a soiled lantern. When the glass protecting the inner flame is covered with soot, the light appears dimmed. As we clear the haze of our hurting and the residues of resentment, the love that we are beams unrestricted. And it is in the radiance of our love that we fulfill the possibility of living in heaven while breathing on earth.

In this higher place of consciousness, loving ourselves and others is both a key to fulfillment and the natural expression of who we are.

WHAT IF—

As we clear the haze of our hurting and the residues of resentment, the light that we are beams unrestricted. And it is in the radiance of our love that we fulfill the possibility of living in heaven while breathing on earth.

WHAT IF—

In this higher place of consciousness, loving ourselves and others is both a key to fulfillment and the natural expression of who we are.

Try It Out Exercise: The Power in Empowerment

On the first night of our LCA Weekend Seminar, we do an exercise called "The Power of Empowerment" that raises the energy in the room to a peak state. In the span of a few hours, total strangers become family. Skepticism and fear transmute into hope and oneness. Over time, this simple practice actually builds participants' ability to create the experience of loving. I'd like to offer the following two exercise options so you can create a similar experience.

Option 1: Empowering Yourself

Empowerment is one of the most powerful tools in our LCA arsenal. This tool is designed to build authentic self-esteem over time. The exercise uses the principle of empowerment to build a vastly more encouraging relationship with one's self. Until we experience love for ourselves, we find ourselves caught up in endless cycles of self-sabotage in all its many forms.

You can go through the following six-step process. Or if you prefer, I'll walk you through the steps in the video titled Empowerment Option 1:
www.lcaproject.com/the-opening-videos

Step 1:

Create for yourself a quiet time and place where you will be uninterrupted. Light a candle and ask with all your heart to experience the loving presence and assistance of God in this exercise, feeling grateful for knowing your prayer is already answered.

Step 2:

Write a list of good qualities about yourself. See if you can begin with a list of at least 20 positive characteristics about you. (Examples may include: I get the job done at work. I'm a good friend. I'm honest. I truly love my kids.) If you need assistance on this, ask a supportive friend to help expand your list.

Step 3:

Normally when we stand in front of a mirror, our focus is on making ourselves look presentable. This exercise requires a different kind of focus. While looking in the mirror deliberately love the being you see reflected back to you.

Who is that incredible person living behind those eyes? Using a timer, speak words of empowerment, out loud, for a minimum of five minutes. Feel free to refer to your list. Consciously and deliberately love the being you see in the mirror without judgment. Allow yourself to be moved by who you are.

As you look deeply into the eyes of this being in the mirror, notice any resistance, skepticism or self judgment and just let it go. Notice your walls of protection. If you feel uncomfortable, hang in there. It's just five minutes. Truly, the more you practice this exercise, the easier and more fulfilling it becomes.

Again, look into the eyes of this incredible being. Notice the walls you have had to build for your protection in an unenlightened and often hostile world. Realize that underneath your need for protection, is your hurt—years and years of hurt. If you look, you will see it.

Step 4:

Now go even deeper. Notice that beneath your hurt is how much you care, and beneath your caring is how much you love. You wouldn't hurt if you didn't care. You wouldn't care if you didn't love.

The eyes are indeed the windows to the soul. As you continue looking into your own eyes, allow yourself to be moved by the profound love that lives in this being. In this place of loving, you can see your very soul. Allow yourself to be moved deeply by this sacred honor. See that all you've ever truly wanted is to love and be loved.

Now allow the love in you to connect and commune with the love in your reflection. And in this communion, experience the oneness. This is the oneness we all are as human beings. Not just some of us. All of us.

Breathe this in. Feel this. Remember this. Practice this.

Step 5:

Take just a moment to say "Thank you" to God for this opportunity to see who lives in every human being.

Step 6:

To maximize the impact of this exercise, please write your answers to the following questions:

What is it like to look into your own eyes and see the very essence of who you are?

_____

_____

_____

_____
_____
_____
_____
_____

What is it like to empower yourself?

_____
_____
_____
_____
_____
_____
_____

How will your relationships be different, knowing that this light of love that lives in you is in every human being?

_____
_____
_____
_____
_____
_____

What would be the value of seeing the magnificence that lives in you as an ongoing practice? Are you willing to do this?

_____
_____
_____

_____

_____

_____

_____

_____

Option 2: Empowering Another

To do this exercise, you will need a partner who is willing to try something a little unusual, someone you trust and who cares about you. Who do you know who might be willing to take a few minutes to make a positive difference in your life?

_____

_____

_____

The following steps will guide you through the process. For this second option of empowering another, it is especially useful for both of you to be guided by the video: Empowerment Option 2.

www.lcaproject.com/the-opening-videos

There are six steps to this exercise. The more you are willing to open your heart and allow yourself to be moved by the power of love, the more value you will receive.

Step 1:

Create for yourself a quiet time and place where you and your partner will not be interrupted. Light a candle and ask with all your heart to experience the loving presence and assistance of God in this exercise, feeling grateful for knowing your prayer is already answered.

Step 2:

Stand facing your partner and share as many of your own positive qualities as you can for a minute or so. That's right—everything that is great about you. Share your talents, abilities, successes. Share how you've positively impacted others and key accomplishments in your life that are a source of pride for you.

I know this is outside the comfort zone for many, but that's where we grow, right? Resist the inclination to go into the negative. For this exercise, share only the good stuff!

Meanwhile, your partner's job is to listen in a particular way; to listen from the heart while consciously focusing on what's wonderful about you.

After a minute or so, switch roles.

Step 3:

Again standing in front of your partner, actually see the beauty in this person. Focus on their virtues, talents and great qualities. Now, just for a minute or two, look in their eyes while telling them specifically and authentically what you appreciate about them. Place zero focus on their faults— 100 percent of your focus on their greatness.

As you do this, their job is to receive your empowerment. So often, in our culture, we discount and minimize compliments from others. That's like going to your employer on payday saying, "Oh no, I couldn't! Why don't you just keep the money this month?"

When we deflect the acknowledgement of others, not only do we rip off ourselves from receiving their gift, we rip off the other person by denying them the satisfaction of contributing to us.

So whoever is on the receiving end of the empowerment has the task of letting in the compliments as deeply as possible. A great way to do this is to simply say inwardly, "Thank you for seeing that in me," then experience gratitude for having been given those particular qualities.

After a minute or so, switch roles.

Step 4:

This next step is done in total silence. Simply look into your partner's eyes and see who's in there. If laughter or silliness comes up, know it's just a way of dealing with the initial discomfort of intimacy. Don't fight it. Just allow the laughter, then come back into the silence.

As you look deeply into the eyes of your partner without speaking, notice their need to protect themselves. Notice their walls of protection.

Then look deeper. Realize that underneath their need for protection, is their hurt. Years and years of hurt. It's not possible to grow up in this culture without being hurt deeply. If you look into the eyes of your partner, you will see it.

Then look even deeper. Notice that beneath their hurt is how much they care and beneath their caring is how much they love. They wouldn't hurt if they didn't care. They wouldn't care if they didn't love.

The eyes are indeed the windows to the soul. As you continue looking into their eyes in silence, allow yourself to be moved by the profound love that they are. In this place of loving, you can see their very soul. Allow yourself to be moved deeply by this sacred honor. See that all they've ever truly wanted is to love and be loved.

Then know that just as you have seen their walls, they have seen yours. Just as you have seen their hurt, they have seen yours as well. Just as you have seen their caring/loving essence, they have seen these qualities in you. And just as you have seen all the way into the soul of another human being, they have witnessed the soul that you are.

Now allow the love in you to connect and commune with the love in your partner. Just be with this person in silence. And in this communion, experience the oneness. Take a moment and savor this gift. This is the oneness we all are as human beings.

Breathe this in. Feel this. Remember this.

Very good. Now when you're ready, just thank your partner and if you both are willing, give each other a hug.

Step 5:

Take just a moment to say, "Thank you" to God for this opportunity to see who lives in every human being.

Step 6:

Briefly write your answers to the following questions as your partner does the same. Then come back together and share your realizations.

What was it like to empower yourself?

_____

_____

_____

_____

_____

_____

_____

What was it like to empower another?

_____
_____
_____
_____
_____
_____
_____
_____
_____
_____
_____
_____

What was it like to be empowered by another person?

_____
_____
_____
_____
_____
_____
_____
_____
_____
_____
_____
_____
_____
_____

How will life be different for you knowing that this light of love is in every human being?

#3 - SURRENDER AND TRUST

I once heard of a simple method for catching monkeys in the wild. A small, wooden box with a few peanuts inside would be secured to the ground. A hole in the top would be just large enough for a monkey's hand to squeeze through.

When a hungry monkey approached the box, it would reach in and grab the peanuts. But now its fist was too big to withdraw from the box. At this point, someone could simply walk up and grab the monkey. This was only possible because rather than let go of the peanuts to gain its freedom, it would hang on to what it so desperately wanted.

Is it possible, in much the same way, that God asks us to "Surrender and Trust" so we too, might attain a new level of liberation?

What does it mean to surrender? Surrender doesn't mean quitting or running away. It is not cowardice, nor does it necessarily mean physically giving away all our possessions. Surrender is a courageous inner experience of releasing. It's about letting go of our hyper-vigilant control. Letting go of our death grip on life. Letting go of our desperate attachment to having things be a certain way.

Releasing Attachment

Understanding the nature of attachment is important because to the extent we're attached to someone (or something) we live in fear of losing what we're attached to. And to the extent we live in fear, we cannot feel love because the experiences of love and fear are also mutually exclusive.

Attachment occurs whenever we find ourselves desperately hanging on to someone or something in order to avoid an unwanted experience (like the pain we would feel if someone left us). Why is this so?

Consider the possibility that love and attachment are actually polar opposites. The hallmark of love is unconditional acceptance and deep appreciation, where attachment is VERY conditional upon things turning out a particular way, and true appreciation is non-existent.

We can be attached to anything: a person (whether they're with us or not), money, success, what people think of us, our cars, having things our way, the well-being of our children, our youth, our life, ANYTHING! And when we become attached, the very thought of losing the subject of our attachment generates tremendous stress, fear and upset.

A good way to understand attachment is to notice how it shows up in relationships. Two people fall in love. They experience mutual unconditional acceptance and deep appreciation. The chemistry is intense and life is grand. Then at some point, one of them becomes attached to the other. They do this by unconsciously declaring their partner to be their primary source of love, joy and fulfillment.

As soon as this happens, the person who is attached becomes dependent upon the other person expressing love in a

74

WHAT IF—

Surrender doesn't mean quitting or running away. It is not cowardice, nor does it necessarily mean physically giving away all our possessions. Surrender is a courageous inner experience of releasing. It's about letting go of our hyper-vigilant control. Letting go of our death grip on life. Letting go of our desperate attachment to having things be a certain way.

WHAT IF—

Understanding the nature of attachment is important because to the extent we're attached to someone (or something) we live in fear of losing what we're attached to. And to the extent we live in fear, we cannot feel love because the experiences of love and fear are mutually exclusive.

particular way. The person who is attached starts clinging and manipulating, which of course drives their partner away. And fast! Then what began as a truly loving relationship, disintegrates into frustration for the cling-ee and agonizing separation for the cling-or.

In our culture, we confuse love and attachment to the point of insanity. Just turn on the TV and watch the drama as relationships reveal their craziness. When we're attached, we have to fight and struggle to hang on. So ultimately, we don't really have the thing we're attached to, so much as it has us.

Let's look at our attachment to money. A recent Harris poll of over 3,000 people revealed that 22 percent of Americans experienced "extreme stress" about money on a regular basis. When we decide that money is the source of our peace, joy and happiness, it makes the threat of losing our funding feels like a threat to our very survival. Our stress level goes through the roof and we pay a price. Of course study after study acknowledges the link between stress and disease.

To live free of attachment requires that we fully embrace a vital distinction. It requires that we know the difference between our challenging circumstances and fear itself. On the deepest level we must know that no circumstance has the power to generate fear. Only our interpretation of circumstances can generate fear. If we truly want a breakthrough in the area of spiritual freedom, consider the possibility that fear—IS NOT—a function of circumstances.

Imagine two men of the same age and salary are employed by the same company. Both individuals have a family to feed and mortgage to pay. A rumor of layoffs begins to spread. The man who is desperately attached to his job feels consumed in fear.

WHAT IF—

In our culture, we confuse love and attachment to the point of insanity. Just turn on the TV and watch the drama as relationships reveal their craziness. When we're attached, we have to fight and struggle to hang on. So ultimately we don't really have the thing we're attached to, so much as it has us.

WHAT IF—

Fear—IS NOT—a function of circumstances.

"I CAN'T get laid off! If I do, I'll never get another job with this pay rate! I'll lose my home! My wife will lose respect for me and leave! My kids will hate me if they have to move!

The other man is unattached. "I sure don't want to lose this job but if it happens, it happens. If this door closes, another will open. In fact, this might be a huge opportunity to expand into something I've always wanted to do!"

Two different people. Same circumstances. One is attached. One is not. If the circumstances had the power to create fear, wouldn't both men be suffering?

How do you know when you are attached? The very thought of losing something brings up instant hurt and upset. So, what are you afraid of losing? Your spouse, your home, your kids, your life?

At this point, you might be thinking, "Wait a minute, Randy, are you nuts? Are you suggesting I give up my attachment to my home, my kids—to the people I love? No way!"

Yes. That's exactly what I'm saying.

You surrender your attachment, not your love. Let go of your fear of losing the people who are dear to you, while doing whatever you can to serve them. Releasing attachment isn't about getting rid of things nor is it about avoiding responsibility. In your actions, you do what works, caring for yourself and the people around you. But in your heart, be willing to lose whatever you have been attached to.

The irony is that our attachment doesn't keep what we're afraid of losing, from leaving. If anything, it drives it away. Attachment invites lessons from the Universe about letting go and discovering what is truly Source.

WHAT IF—

You surrender your attachment, not your love.

Suffering comes from resisting what is. In our culture we resist what is, in epidemic proportions. We operate under the premise, "My will be done on earth as it is in heaven." This creates a life of anxiously having to manipulate circumstances to get what we want. It's like swimming up a waterfall. Very effortful.

Learning to Surrender

Until we surrender to the truth, our vision will be clouded by the way we demand things to be. By insisting that things be different from the way they are in the moment, we are sprinting down the track blindfolded. Very disorienting. It's like being in Los Angeles with a roadmap of Boston.

Surrender means accepting life exactly the way it is—the way God has it in this instant. The opportunity is to then move forward, taking appropriate action. It's a life that flows with the river instead of against it.

Consider the possibility that God truly is all-powerful. If that is the case, His will is always done. Always. Can you picture God waking up one morning, looking out into the Universe and saying, "I HATE IT when that happens!" Not very likely.

Isn't it far more probable that everything is exactly as God wills it in every moment? And this includes mankind having to face the consequences of eons of living lower on the Wisdom Curve.

Surrender operates under the premise: "Thy will be done on earth as it is in heaven." This is about cooperating with the way things are. When we surrender our will to God's will, then our will is always done as well. Much less effortful. Much more rewarding.

WHAT IF—

Suffering comes from resisting what is.

WHAT IF—

*Surrender means accepting life exactly the way it is—
the way God has it in this instant. The opportunity is
to then move forward, taking appropriate action.
It's a life that flows with the river
instead of against it.*

Can you recall a time when you were stressed to the max, then consciously decided to let go of your attachment? Inwardly you said, "I don't like it but if I lose it, I lose it." The instant you did this, how did you feel inside? Didn't you feel a sense of peace? And what happened to your ability to see clearly the actions you needed to take?

Didn't your clarity improve dramatically? What you did was surrender. What got restored was your peace, vision and dignity.

Often, the moment you truly surrender an attachment, you will feel a sadness come up inside yourself. The key to mastery over hurt is the willingness to experience it fully. Feel your hurt deliberately and purposefully because you choose to. Reach in, grab it and pull it out like children do so masterfully. Just like Emily, cry if you can. The harder, the better.

When I take clients through this healing exercise and ask them afterwards, "How does that feel?" their most frequent reply is a single word, "Lighter." They feel like a huge weight has been lifted. This is surrender in action.

Yet, surrender is not about being a doormat. It's not about being weak or giving up. It's about letting go, creating peace and clarity within, then courageously taking right action.

Hank's mom was an alcoholic. She was a mean drunk and Hank had the emotional scars that come with that kind of upbringing. In adulthood he continued to fight with her almost every time they got together.

Then she died suddenly. Hank never got to make peace with her or even say goodbye. In his guilt, he spiraled downward, repeating much of the behavior his mom had modelled.

Years later, I worked with Hank to release his resentment for

WHAT IF—

Surrender is not about being a doormat.
It's not about being weak or giving up.
It's about letting go, creating peace and clarity within,
then courageously taking right action.

how he'd been treated and his guilt for not being there for his mom when she passed. It was only then that Hank realized how he loved her, but now it was too late to tell her. He was still miserable.

The last major step came in releasing his attachment to her. For even though Hank's mom had been gone for years, he still longed for her. He was still attached.

We used one of the LCA tools, a Gestalt exercise, where he imagined being with his mother. Once again, he got to speak with her. Any vestige of past judgment gave way to intense compassion. They made their peace. Then he consciously and deliberately released her. In that moment, years of hurt from intimacy lost, came up to be healed. He cried hard, breathed deeply and then got on with the business of creating a great life. Then whenever he thought of his mom, he just smiled.

So, to what or to whom have you been attached?

Are you willing to surrender, to release your attachment, to let any hurt come and go and to feel the resulting peace? The greater your surrender, the more peaceful you feel, the more available you are to God's guidance, the more life works.

We're not taking anything with us when we go, are we? When was the last time you saw a hearse pulling a U-Haul? So, the opportunity in surrender is to—

Let go. Let go. Let go.

I believe it was Thoreau who said, "A man is rich in proportion to the number of things which he can afford to let alone."

WHAT IF—

We're not taking anything with us when we go,
are we?
When was the last time you saw a hearse
pulling a U-Haul?
So, the opportunity in surrender is to—
Let go. Let go. Let go.

WHAT IF—

"A man is rich in proportion to the number of things
which he can afford to let alone."
– Henry Thoreau

Surrendering to God

What does it mean to surrender to God?

Quite simply, it means giving up your attachment to life itself. From the bottom of your heart, it's giving Him everything. Your possessions. Your destiny. Your loved ones. Your body. Your free will. Your very life.

Why in the world would you want to do such a thing?

When you give your life to God, a quantum shift in consciousness takes place. It's as if your entire life has been lived in black and white, and now you live in color. Before, you had to figure it all out yourself. You were separate and had to "make it" on your own.

Now you are intimately partnered with the wisest, most powerful, most loving beingness in the Universe. You discover that there is nothing you can ever do to earn God's love—because you've never had to. He just loves you—completely. Infinitely. Unconditionally. Always and forever.

This means there's nothing you have to do to prove your value. In the realm of action, you continue to do what works. In the realm of the heart, you've already won the race and are now home free. How does that feel?

When you surrender your life to God, you begin living in an entirely different way. In this sacred relationship your humility becomes an opening for divine counsel. Ironically, in surrendering your attachment to life—you do not lose yourself. You find yourself. You discover on a profound level that you and God are made of the same material. You know that who you are—the soul that you are—cannot be hurt. You live in the world but are not of the world.

WHAT IF—

There is nothing you can ever do
to earn God's love.
Why? Because you've never had to.
He just loves you completely.
Infinitely. Unconditionally.
Always and forever.

You experience a oneness that manifests in true freedom.

When you surrender your life to God, you're let in on two cosmic jokes. First, think for a moment, how much of your precious life energy have you spent trying to arrange and accumulate circumstances in order to feel happy, loved and respected? Like a fish in the ocean searching for water or a bird in flight, questing for air—we yearn for that sense of belonging, which is the truth of who we already are.

Imagine—What good might you do with all that freed up energy?

The second cosmic joke has to do with ownership. Since, clearly, we are not taking anything with us when we go, at best, we are just temporary stewards. All we "possess" is just on loan to us for a little while. I mean, what doesn't belong to the Creator of the Universe?

Living with this perspective allows us to shift our focus from "having to get" to "getting to have." We shift from life happening to us, to life happening for us.

When you surrender your life to God, you feel enveloped in infinite love and know what it means to be truly alive. You know that there is nothing you can ever do to jeopardise this truth no matter how hard you try. The instant

WHAT IF—

Surrendering allows us to shift our focus from
"having to get" to "getting to have."
We shift from life happening to us,
to life happening for us.

you surrender in this way, the universe whispers tenderly, "Welcome back."

In the midst of the U.S. Civil war, Abraham Lincoln was invited to a prayer breakfast with a group of ministers. Although Lincoln seldom attended church, he was certainly a man of deep faith.

During the meeting, one of the ministers spoke up saying, "Let us pray that God is on our side." To which Lincoln replied, "No, my friend, let us pray that we are on God's side."

Try It Out Exercise: Learning to Surrender

To move to a beautiful place of inner freedom, surrender and connection with God, go through the following steps or allow me to guide you through the video: Learning To Surrender.

www.lcaproject.com/the-opening-videos

This exercise takes you through the steps of releasing attachment. The assumption for this exercise is that you are attached to a person. If you are attached to a thing or an outcome, just go ahead and alter the wording in a way that works for you. The principle is the same.

Here's a vital key to maximizing the value. If you go through these steps on a mental level, the impact will be marginal. If you go through these steps from a place deep in your heart, you will create a level of freedom that is uncommon in the world.

Step 1:

The evidence of attachment is that the very thought of losing this person is extremely painful. So specifically, who are you most afraid of losing? To whom are you attached?

_____
_____
_____
_____
_____
_____
_____
_____
_____
_____

Step 2:

Create for yourself a quiet time and place where you will be uninterrupted. Light a candle and ask with all your heart to experience the loving presence and assistance of God in this exercise, feeling grateful for knowing your prayer is already answered.

Step 3:

Remember, the objective is to release your attachment, not your love. Notice what your clinging and hanging on has cost you. Consider the areas of your joy, your self-esteem, your relationships, your personal dignity, your effectiveness, your ability to set boundaries, your being present with the people in your life. What price have you paid in being attached?

Step 4:

Also notice that your hanging on has had the exact opposite effect that you want. The more you cling, the more you push the person away, live in fear, and invite a lesson from the Universe about surrender.

Step 5:

The antidote to attachment is being totally willing to lose the subject of your attachment. In this case, it is the person you have most feared losing. This isn't about telling this person to leave, it's about being totally willing for whatever is going to happen, to happen. In your heart, you give them complete permission to go.

Willingness is a choice. Now, from the deepest part of your heart, are you willing to release your attachment? Are you willing to lose this person? Fortunately, you don't have to like it in order to be free. It may simply sound like, "I don't like it one bit, but yes, I'm willing."

If you notice a reluctance at this point to be willing, you might ask yourself, "How effective has my attachment been in keeping them around?" Then notice that attachment itself doesn't do anything but damage.

Step 6:

Once you're willing, there are some very powerful words you can use to release this person. Again, from the depths of your heart, say (and mean) the words:

"God, I give _____ to you."
"God, I give _____ to you— forever."

Step 7:

At this point you may experience some sadness, loss or hurt. Let the tears come fully to the best of your ability. Cry hard if you can. This is a vital step. This sadness is the energetic glue that has kept your attachment in place. So, let the hurt come and go like a child. It's OK to let the sadness leave your body. Take a moment for yourself and do this now.

Step 8:

When you have released your attachment experientially, notice how it feels inside. What does it feel like to let go, *to be free of your attachment?*

Step 9:

Now take this experience to an even higher level. If you are willing, give your life to God. Surrender your addiction to "making it" in the world. Offer all of you to the One who loves you, the One who created you. From the depths of your heart, say and mean the words:

"God, I give myself to you."
"God, I give myself to you—forever."

Step 10:

Very good. Now breathe that in, and when you're ready, jot down your answers to the following questions:

What was it like for you to release your attachment, to truly surrender?

What was it like for you to give your life to God?

_____

_____

_____

_____

_____

_____

Step 11:

Take a moment to express gratitude for receiving what your soul has been yearning for—a beautiful prayer, beautifully answered.

Learning to Trust

When God first spoke to me of trust, I had no idea how vital a role it plays in our well-being. Truly, I can be a little slow on the uptake sometimes.

Years ago in my Masters program at USM, we were all guided through a special meditation, the purpose of which was to come up with a key word to inspire us throughout the academic year. Afterward, we had the opportunity to share our experience in the group.

Instead of going into my heart for the answer, I made the mistake of listening to my ego. When Dr. Mary Hulnick called on me, I stood up and shared my key word: "Power!" At this, the room went politely silent as if my classmates sensed I was waaaaay off base.

Of course, Dr. Hulnick sensed this as well and asked me, "Randy, what happened in your meditation?"

I responded, "Well, Jesus was standing in front of a giant white board. He was holding a bucket of bright purple paint in one hand and a large paint brush in the other. Then he began writing on the board in huge letters: T - R - U - S - T."

In the midst of stifled laughter, Dr. Hulnick asked me with the kindness and compassion that's become her hallmark, "Randy, is it possible your key word might be—Trust?"

In our culture, we drastically undervalue trust. What I've come to discover is that if we want to restore ourselves to an inspired, joyful, spiritual life, learning to trust is HUGE!

Why Trusting is So Vital

To the extent we do not trust, we live in fear. To the extent we live in fear, we are frantic to control. To the extent we are frantic to control, we cannot allow what is. To the extent we cannot allow what is, we cannot accept and appreciate. To the extent we cannot accept and appreciate, we cannot experience love. As I shared before, it is impossible in the moment to experience both love and fear. At any given instant, it's one or the other—but not both.

We're taught that our ability to trust is determined by the behavior of the people and circumstances around us. If people and circumstances around us behave the way we want them to, then we think we can trust. If they don't, we can't.

But if we operate that way, to whom or what are we giving away all our power to trust? That's right—to the people and circumstances around us. Well, that just doesn't work very well, does it?

To reclaim our ability to trust, there are three key realizations to take in deeply.

Realization 1: I Can Live Free of Fear. Consider the possibility that the root emotion of anxiety, worry, terror and stress—is fear. To conquer fear is to rid yourself of these tremendous energy drains. Just imagine how will life be without these life-force leeches?

Try this one on. Fear is created in our unwillingness to experience something. The more we are unwilling to experience something, the greater our fear. The more we create the willingness to experience the subject of our fear, the more our fear disappears. Isn't this the key dynamic that heals attachment – experiencing the release of whoever or whatever we have been hanging onto?

Remember grade school? What happens when you run from the bully? Does he or she just give up or do they continue their taunting? But when you finally muster the courage to face your oppressor, what happens?

Terri had been assisting in our seminars for years. In one of our weekend events, she let it slip out that she had an absolute terror of spiders. In the instant that followed we could all see the utter panic on her face because she knew I would ask if she wanted to be free of her fear.

It would have been fine if Terri had said no, because all of our activities are done with deep respect for our participants' free will. To her great credit though, she chose to proceed. She had become sick and tired of being run by her phobia.

Terri shared that her terror was so intense that if a little spider made an appearance in her home, she would bolt out the door and call her husband. He would have to leave work, come home and remove the visitor from the premises. Only then could Terri go back inside.

So with her permission, I asked Terri to fully allow what she had been so fiercely resisting. I asked her to imagine being locked in a room with a spider. Immediately, she began to shake and tears welled up in her eyes.

After struggling a minute or so, she let go, took a deep breath and fully allowed herself to be in a room with a spider. Then she asked, "Are we done?" I asked her if her fear had lifted and she replied, "A little."

WHAT IF—

To the extent we do not trust, we live in fear.
To the extent we live in fear,
we are frantic to control.
To the extent we are frantic to control,
we cannot allow what is.
To the extent we cannot allow what is,
we cannot accept and appreciate.
To the extent we cannot accept and appreciate,
we cannot experience love.

WHAT IF—

Fear is created in our unwillingness to
experience something.
The more we are unwilling to experience
something, the greater our fear.
The more we create the willingness to
experience the subject of our fear,
the more our fear disappears.

I said, "OK, now I want you to imagine that the spider comes over to you and begins to crawl up your arm."

Terri said, "No! That's too much!" but quickly caught herself and said, "Let's keep going. I want to get rid of this."

Again, Terri cried as her body shook. After another deep breath, once more she courageously allowed the situation and said, "OK, I HATE THIS, but yes, I'm willing. Are we done yet?"

When asked again if the fear was gone, she replied, "Almost."

Then I said, "There's just one more step. Now I want you to imagine the absolute worst-case scenario. Imagine that your entire body is covered with venomous spiders, biting you to the point of death."

Terri looked at me like I was insane, closed her eyes, and one more time cried hard as she fully allowed the worst. When she released the last tear, she took one more deep breath, came present with us once again and smiled. The fear had completely disappeared.

About six months later I asked her how she was doing with the spider issue. She beamed and replied, "Oh I'm doing great. If I see a spider I just catch it, give it a name and release it in the back yard."

What Terri had demonstrated so masterfully was that when we become willing in our hearts for the worst to happen, we actually dismantle the mechanism of fear.

Please note here, "being willing" and "intending" are two very different things. In no way was Terri intending that she be surrounded by spiders. She simply became willing to allow for the possibility that the worst could happen.

WHAT IF—

*When we become willing in our hearts
for the worst to happen, we actually
dismantle the mechanism of fear.*

WHAT IF—
*"Being willing" and "intending"
are two very different things.*

Have you ever had a fear of something happening, then said to yourself, "If it happens, it happens? Somehow I'll get to the other side." How did that feel? So in your heart, you let go. In your actions, you do what works.

What is the number one fear you have that has kept you from trusting?

What would happen to your fear if deep within your heart you faced the worst case scenario and gave it total permission to happen?

In prayer, it might sound like this: God, I surrender. I let go. I ask that this challenge be lifted from me, but You know far better than I do what is best in the long run. If it's your will that this event I have been resisting actually happens, then let it be so. God, I'm willing. I trust.

Realization 2: I Really CAN Trust. It's important to know that you can completely trust every single human being and every single circumstance on the planet, 100 percent of the time, 24/7. Sound crazy? It's true.

You can count on every single person and every single circumstance - to be EXACTLY the way they are. This, you can trust.

Think about THE person you have the most difficulty with in your life. Isn't that person EXACTLY the way they are? Aren't they that way whether you like it or not? They're that way and you can absolutely trust that.

The real question is, can you trust YOURSELF to relate to the people and circumstances in your life effectively, given they are the way they are? The higher you grow up the Wisdom Curve, the more capable you become in relating to anyone and everything.

WHAT IF—

*What would happen to your fear if deep within
your heart you faced the worst case scenario
and gave it total permission to happen?*

WHAT IF—

*God, I surrender. I let go. I ask that this challenge
be lifted from me, but You know far better than I do
what is best in the long run. If it's your will
that this event I have been resisting
actually happens, then let it be so.
God, I'm willing. I trust.*

WHAT IF—

*It's important to know that you can completely trust
every single human being on the planet 100 percent
of the time, 24/7. You can count on every single person
and every single circumstance - to be EXACTLY the
way they are. This, you can trust.*

Realization 3: I've Always Been Cared For. Every moment of your life, you've been given exactly what you have needed to grow. Certainly, you haven't always received what you've wanted, but you have ALWAYS received what you needed to evolve as a being. Even in your toughest moments, haven't you been given what was required to make it through?

In seminars I ask the question, "For how many of you, have your most difficult times brought you your most important lessons?" Again, most every hand is raised. So consider the possibility that with great love, and in every instant of your life, you have been brought the people and circumstances required to grow you perfectly for your own unique life curriculum. For the rest of your life, you can absolutely trust this dynamic to be true.

There is tremendous value in living moment to moment, knowing that you—especially and uniquely you—are completely known, loved and continually cared for. Even at the moment of death, when your spirit leaves the body, who you are will be totally and completely provided for. Notice, what does it feel like to be loved this much? You might want to really let this in.

I recall a particular experience walking with my brother in New Jersey on a brisk autumn evening. He was showing me the proper way to hold a cigarette. What a cool older brother!

However, the most meaningful part of this memory was just being with him on our walks. I had a sense that as long as I was with my big brother, all was well.

After all, he was 15 and knew everything. He would guide me and care for me. The rest of the world didn't matter.

These days, I get that same feeling of security and being on

WHAT IF—

*You haven't always received what you've wanted,
but you have ALWAYS received what you
needed to evolve as a being.*

track when I experience trusting in my partnership with God (who by the way is a much better influence).

A Little Side Benefit of Trusting – Freedom From Worry Forever

What is the number one area of your life that is a bit troublesome, that has been a source of stress and worry for you?

_____

_____

_____

_____

Now consider for a moment that anytime you worry, there are two distinct pieces to the problem. The first piece is entirely external. It is the situation, the people and the circumstances.

The second piece of the problem is entirely internal. It is what is taking place inside of you; your thoughts and emotions.

Do you see that these are two very separate realms, the external and the internal? And can you guess in which realm worry lives? Of course, it lives entirely in the internal realm.

Do you also see that there is a huge difference between worry and being attentive? It is the difference between being vigilant which is paying attention in a healthy way, and being hyper-vigilant which is an entirely fear-based reaction.

So, consider the possibility that worry itself has no value whatsoever. In fact, it dramatically restricts our field of possibilities and makes us far less capable in handling the challenge. Bottom line: WORRY DOESN'T WORK. Its only value is in revealing the opportunity to let go and trust. And this is true regardless of the severity of the challenge.

From the Bible, Mathew 6:27 – "Can any of you by worrying, add a single hour to your life?"

With these realizations, trusting becomes a choice. Choose the path of worry and you get all the outcomes that come with a fearful state of being. Choose the path of trusting and you get all the outcomes that come with love.

In the course of our LCA Weekend, the seminar walls literally become covered with flipcharts expressing key realizations. One of my favorites that pertains to worry, is this: "We have freedom of choice but we do not have freedom of consequences."

So, the opportunity here is to choose. Fear or trust? How would it feel to make and maintain the inner declaration:

"For the rest of my life, I never ever, ever, ever have to worry again!"

You might take just a moment and breathe into this realization. How does THAT feel?When we embrace the first three invitations of the Sacred Six, we discover:

To the extent we experience love, we live free of judgment.

To the extent we experience surrender, we live free of attachment.

To the extent we experience trust, we live free of fear.

So are you willing to love, to unconditionally accept and appreciate? Are you willing to surrender, to give yourself the freedom that comes from releasing the bondage of attachment? And are you willing to banish that thief named fear who steals your peace and robs your joy—by choosing to trust?

Consider the notion that you did not create yourself. Consider the idea that your life—your presence here on the planet—your ability to read and comprehend this sentence right now —your next breath—all are creations, amazing gifts from a Higher Source.

If this is true, what will be the value in having a beautiful ongoing relationship with this Divine Provider? What will be the value of living from moment to moment, knowing that you—especially and uniquely you—are completely known, infinitely loved and continually cared for?

What difference will this make over a lifetime?

WHAT IF—

*To the extent we experience love,
we live free of judgment.
To the extent we experience surrender,
we live free of attachment.
To the extent we experience trust,
we live free of fear.*

Try It Out Exercise: The Gift of Trusting

Imagine for a moment that you are a participant in one of our seminars. I ask for a volunteer and you are kind enough to step forward.

Standing behind you, I ask you to keep your body straight and to lean back. As I catch you, I slowly begin to lean you back even further. At this point if I were to let go, you would not be able to break your fall.

I tell you that at any moment, I might just walk away. Then I ask you to tell me who I am.

You reply, "A sadist?"

My answer is, "Nope. I'm the people and circumstances in your life. How are you feeling by the way?"

You say, "Very nervous."

I say, "Welcome to your life, where well-being is dependent on people and things. Would you be interested in an alternative?"

You respond emphatically, "Yes!"

I lift you up and we walk over to a very solid wall. Again, I ask you to lean back against it. You do so and again I ask, "How are you feeling?"

You say, "This is much better."

I ask, "Why?"

"Because this wall isn't going anywhere. Unlike you, I can depend on it."

I say, "Welcome to your life, where well-being is dependent upon an all-knowing, all-powerful, all present, all-loving, all-available being who like you say, "isn't going anywhere."

I love this USM quote. They say: "The willingness to do creates the ability to do." If you're not willing, most likely it's not going to happen. If you are willing, the opening is there for meaningful change.

So the question is quite simple. Are you willing to experience trusting something you can absolutely trust? Here's an exercise that might help. To experience this exercise on video, go to:

www.lcaproject.com/the-opening-videos

Then select the video: The Gift of Trusting

Step 1:

Create for yourself a quiet time and place where you will be uninterrupted. Light a candle and ask with all your heart to experience the loving presence and assistance of God in this exercise, feeling grateful for knowing your prayer is already answered.

Step 2:

Recall for a moment, what was the most difficult and painful time of your life?

_____

_____

_____

_____

_____

Step 3:

What are a few of the most significant lessons you learned in moving through this challenge?

_____

_____

_____

_____

_____

_____

Step 4:

In what ways have these lessons grown you up the Wisdom Curve and fashioned you into a better human being?

_____

_____

_____

_____

_____

_____

_____

Step 5:

Now, here are a series of "willingness" questions I would like to ask to enhance your ability to trust—from my heart to yours:

- *Are you willing to shift your definition of reality from what is provable to what is useful?*

- *Are you willing to embrace a reality in which there <u>really is</u> an all-knowing, all-powerful, all-present, all-available, all-loving Beingness that is orchestrating life* *and this amazing physical Universe?*

- *Are you willing to open your heart to the possibility that you are absolutely, unconditionally, known and loved beyond measure by this Higher Power—that you are now invited to live in relationship with this Divine Beingness?*

- *Are you willing to accept this invitation?*

- *Are you willing to surrender your attachments to having life be a certain way so you can be guided to even higher possibilities?*

- *Are you willing to dismantle all the expressions of fear by allowing in your heart, for the worst to happen?*

- *Are you willing to acknowledge that the entire planet, and all the activity and people on it (including you) are exactly the way they are, moment by moment, whether you like it or not—and this is something you can trust?*

- *Are you willing to acknowledge that from a place of infinite love, God has consistently brought you (and all humanity) one lesson after another to grow you up the Wisdom Curve and that all the challenges you currently face, are simply your current lesson plan?*

- *Are you willing to consider that as difficult as it's sometimes been, you've made it through every single difficulty—that you have not always received what you've wanted, but you have <u>always</u> received what you've needed to grow?*

- *Are you willing to see that you have always been phenomenally cared for in this way, just as you are in this very moment, and that you always will be?*

- *Are you willing for life to be the way it is—for whatever is going to happen, to happen—committed to taking right action, to do the best you can, as a fallible human being?*

- *Are you willing to live in the declaration: "For the rest of my life, I never ever, ever, ever have to worry again!"*

- *Are you willing to trust?*

- *Are you willing to breathe-in this beautiful gift of trusting?*

Step 6:

Great! Jotting down your answers to the following questions may really help maximize the impact of this exercise.

What does it feel like to really trust?

_____

_____

_____

_____

_____

_____

_____

_____

_____

_____

_____

_____

_____

_____

_____

What happens to your fear as you deliberately, consciously experience trusting?

_____

_____

_____

_____

_____

_____

_____

_____

_____

_____

_____

_____

_____

_____

_____

How will your personal effectiveness be impacted over time as you live in this state of trust?

_____

_____

_____

_____

_____

_____

_____

_____

_____

_____

What else are you discovering about trust?

_____
_____
_____
_____
_____
_____
_____
_____
_____
_____
_____
_____
_____
_____
_____
_____
_____
_____
_____
_____
_____
_____

Step 7:

Thank God for assisting you in reclaiming a new level of new freedom.

#4 - LISTEN AND FOLLOW YOUR GUIDANCE

Imagine you've applied for a job that you want intensely. The interviewer promised to call you today before 2pm. That was three hours ago. By now, you're noticing how attached you've been to a particular outcome. Just as you prepare to release your attachment, you notice your phone has been turned off since breakfast.

Similarly, have you ever prayed to God and heard absolutely nothing in return? Wouldn't it be easy to conclude that God wasn't listening or He didn't care or didn't even exist? But what if the real issue lies in our capacity to hear? What if our spiritual phone has been turned off without our even knowing it? Consider the possibility that until we love, surrender and trust—it's VERY difficult to hear God's guidance. There's just too much static on the line.

How Do We Hear God?

When we are in the experience of love, it is the closest thing we have to a direct line to God. This is because He speaks to us through the realm of the heart. When our hearts are closed, God can feel a million miles away. Do you know that feeling? When our hearts are open, we can feel His presence and the line is open, too.

When we are in a state of surrender, we are open to hearing

and willing to be guided. In a state of attachment, we feel threatened and hang on too tightly to our circumstances to be led to higher possibilities. When we let go of having to do things our way, we can be guided to hear possibilities well outside our current limited reality.

When we are trusting, we know that we are profoundly cared for. In this state of consciousness, there is no fear to inhibit our listening. We can hear our guidance clearly and proceed with confidence. We move forward knowing we are doing exactly the right thing in partnership with God. And what a great feeling that is!

Once we have experientially accomplished these first three steps of the Sacred Six, and the interference on our phone begins to clear, something wonderful opens up to us. We can now enter into conversation and actually experience two-way communication with God. I mean, Wow! This is quite amazing when you think about it.

Listening From the Heart

So how do we turn on our phone?

We increase our capacity to listen—in a whole new way.

Have you ever noticed that there are different kinds of listening? Normally, we consider listening to have occurred if we can repeat accurately what someone has said. But consider the possibility there is a far grander kind of listening. Have you ever been in the presence of someone who listened to you from their heart? Without saying a word—just in the way they listened to you—you felt a foot taller.

By now you know how much I love and respect my brother, Bill. My sister, Jan, is not one iota less amazing.

WHAT IF—

Until we love, surrender and trust—
it's VERY difficult to hear God's guidance.
There's just too much static on the line.

WHAT IF—

When we are in the experience of love,
it is the closest thing we have
to a direct line to God.

She is simply one of the best listeners I've ever met. Jan has a way of listening that can melt your heart. Without speaking a word, she creates a safe place for genuine, meaningful conversation.

From a place of unconditional acceptance and deep appreciation, Jan listens in a way that people truly experience being heard. And they leave the conversation feeling enormously validated.

What is it like to be listened to in this way? What is it like when we listen to others from this depth of caring? What happens when the heart is closed and our listening is purely on the mental level?

In 1989 I spent about six months in Houston, learning how Brother Bill leads his workshops. When I returned to Denver, I was graciously allowed to live in the home of a dear friend. After I got back on my feet financially, I gave her a perfunctory thank you and moved out.

Afterwards, I thought it odd whenever I bumped into my former host, that she would say, "You know, Randy, I never felt appreciated for allowing you to stay in my home."

I would instantly reply, "Don't you remember? I said thank you." She would shake her head, walk away and I would wonder what was wrong with her. After this happened several times, it occurred to me there might be a lesson here—something God was trying to tell me.

I went back to my friend and said, "I don't think I've been listening to you very well. What have you been trying to tell me that I haven't been hearing?"

She looked right at me and practically shouted,

"RANDY, I DIDN'T FEEL APPRECIATED!!!"

This time I didn't resist what she was trying to tell me. I moved from a place of understanding her communication, to a place of listening from my heart. I apologized for taking her generosity for granted. I thanked her profusely for graciously allowing me to live in her home. I told her how meaningful that time was to me, and I meant every word.

She smiled, thanked me for hearing her at last and that was the end of it.

The lesson I learned from my friend was enormous. I learned that at any given instant I am either listening from my mind or listening from my heart. What I hear depends on where I listen FROM. If I want to hear God, I must listen from my heart.

Creating the EXPERIENCE of Love

At this point, you may be thinking, "Great, Randy. How do I actually DO that?" To answer this question, let's look even more deeply at this thing called "love."

In the LCA, we share the possibility that love is so much more than mere emotion. What if love is actually a dimension of life that co-exists with our physical Universe; a dimension we can consciously access, that opens us to authentic, heart-centered listening?

Imagine for a moment that you are doing what you normally do in our physical Universe, just walking along minding your own business, when you notice an unusual gate.

On a whim you step through the gate—and everything changes. The instant you walk through this opening, you feel more love than you ever have in your life. Although the physical Universe remains unaltered, you notice that you are experiencing the world differently. You are experiencing a euphoria that comes with unconditional acceptance and profound appreciation. Your joy knows no limits and is not determined by the circumstances in your life.

Now, in the spirit of experimentation, you step back through the gate. Again, the physical Universe has not changed, but by contrast, you return to a life of relatively little love, a life primarily run by thinking and doing.

No one side of the gate is better than the other. They are just different dimensions co-existing with the physical. However, in experiencing both sides, your awareness has expanded dramatically. You have had an awakening of sorts, which offers awesome new options.

Listening from the heart requires that we consciously step into the love side of the gate. This is a skill—an important one. One way to enter the love side of the gate, is to recall a time when you were deeply moved by your love for someone. Who did you love so profoundly? It might have been a quiet moment as you watched a child in slumber or the warmth you felt saying goodbye to someone special at the airport. Who did you love so deeply and what did it feel like to be on the love side of the gate?

_____

_____

_____

_____

Now it's time to re-create that experience deliberately. The key to creating the experience of love—to consciously step through to the love side of the gate—is to intentionally give the gift of unconditional acceptance and deep appreciation. So deliberately, right now in this moment, imagine extending the gift of unconditional acceptance and deep appreciation to

WHAT IF—

At any given instant I am either listening
from my mind or listening from my heart.
What I hear depends on where I listen FROM.
If I want to hear God, I must listen from my heart.

WHAT IF—

Love is so much more than mere emotion.
What if love is actually a dimension that
co-exists with our physical Universe;
a dimension we can consciously access,
that opens us to authentic, heart-centered listening?

WHAT IF—

The key to creating the experience of love is to
consciously give the gift of unconditional
acceptance and deep appreciation.

someone in your life. Do this intensely. Consciously stoke the furnace of your loving.

Right now in this moment, who is the person you choose to love?

_____

What do you really appreciate about this person? Now open your heart even more. What else do you cherish about this person?

_____
_____
_____
_____
_____
_____
_____

Now, take another moment and really feel how much you love this person. Powerfully and unconditionally accept and appreciate this being. Really ramp it up! How does it feel to deliberately and consciously create love?

_____
_____
_____
_____
_____

In this higher state of consciousness, you have intentionally stepped through to the love side of the gate. This is the domain where heart-centered listening resides.

Sometimes it gets tough out there. Can you recall a time when you had a challenge that was so enormous, it didn't seem to have a viable solution? From this state of upset and confusion, have you ever sought the counsel of a wise friend? And as a result, did you discover solutions you hadn't considered before? Consider the possibility that God is the source of more wisdom than we can possibly conceive.

Accessing Vast Wisdom

Imagine for a moment, an enormous hanging tapestry. This amazing work of art is 50 miles high and 100 miles wide. Now imagine an art critic standing only 4 inches away from this astounding weaving. From his limited vantage point, the colors and patterns may seem senseless and out of balance. Only by stepping back—WAY back—can the critic appreciate the magnificence and majesty of this creation.

In the same way, is it possible that we make decisions about life from an extremely limited perspective? The daily news shares the horrors du jour and life seems totally chaotic. But what if there's a greater plan going on? What if there's a way of navigating through life by listening directly to the Creator of this massive artistic expression?

What will be the value in engaging in ongoing, heart-centered listening with the One who truly knows? What would change in your life if you listened to God in this way and why is this so important? In our heart-centered listening, we can hear what God is trying to tell us sooner rather than later. Just imagine the difference this is going to make over time.

How does one listen to God? Step through to the love side of the gate into a safe space, a place of silence. Be still and listen. As the psalmist wrote,

"Be still and know that I am God."
– Psalm 46:10

In this realm of the heart, you can ask and begin to receive clear, specific, uncommon wisdom. Later, I will share some ideas on how to do this by creating and using your own God Journal.

WHAT IF—

There is a greater plan going on.
What if there's a way of navigating through
life by listening directly to the Creator
of this massive artistic expression?

Try It Out Exercise: Listening to God

Step 1:

Create for yourself a quiet time and place where you will be uninterrupted. Light a candle and ask with all your heart to experience the loving presence and assistance of God in this exercise, feeling grateful for knowing your prayer is already answered.

Step 2:

If you prefer that I guide you, just go to the video below titled: Listening to God.

www.lcaproject.com/the-opening-videos

Step 3:

What is a question you would love to ask God? Go ahead and write it down here:

_____

_____

_____

_____

_____

_____

Step 4:

Breathe deeply and allow your eyes to gently close. Now imagine yourself in the center of a beautiful translucent dome, perhaps 20 feet in diameter, made of billions of angelic prisms. As you sit comfortably, you feel utterly and completely protected. Nothing can harm you in any way. You are infinitely safe. Notice how the light in this dome dances around you.

Savoring each breath, you begin to experience a sacred light swirling and churning just a couple of feet above you. It's as if there was a miniature galaxy of stars glimmering, turning round and round. Now see this sacred light move right into the center of your being. As this magnificent vibrant light continues to circulate within you, it heals everything it touches. Every cell of your body is totally healthy, totally and completely alive. Immersed in this radiance, you feel wholeness, a peace and a joy far beyond anything you have ever experienced.

In this ecstatic place, fully allow an enormous smile on your face. Never have you felt so grateful, so content, so connected to the beauty of the Universe.

Very good. Now, in this state of bliss, imagine walking along the perfect beach. The sun caresses your shoulders as waves crash, sending sound and spray to you in moist embraces. The sand beneath your feet greets your every step, inviting you forward. The colors, the taste and fragrance of ocean air, the palms, the sea grass and azure horizon, are the epitome of nature's beauty. All your senses now embrace this pristine banquet of creation.

In the distance you witness a most extraordinary cloud of light. Formless at first, this intense white light begins to take the shape of another very special being. The closer you come to this angelic form, the more love you feel. And just when you didn't think you could possibly be more joyful, you feel your heart soar beyond words' ability to describe. You are now experiencing just a taste of something we call heaven.

As you look into the eyes of this being of light, you are overwhelmed by the majesty of pure and limitless love. In the same instant, you feel completely known, welcomed and invited into conversation.

This is your opportunity to ask Infinite Wisdom whatever questions you desire. This is your time, so go ahead and recall the question you would most like to ask God. Take this moment to ask for guidance.

"Precious Spirit, what is Your answer to my question? What insight can You provide? What do You want me to learn? How do You want me to proceed?"

Then listen with all your heart. Just be still and listen.

Great. Now, before you return to the physical, what else do you want to learn from this all-knowing, all-present, all-powerful, all-loving, all-available being? Share anything you want. Ask anything you want. And listen.

Now, say good bye for now, keeping this ecstatic relation-ship right in your heart, carrying it with you wherever you go, knowing you can access it any time you choose.

And when you're ready, prepare to come back into your world. Notice your physical surroundings and open your eyes.

Great. Welcome back.

Step 5:

As you keep this sense of spiritual warmth in your heart, take a moment now and just say thank you for the miracle of receiving divine guidance.

Step 6:

Take a few moments and write your answers to the following questions:

What guidance did you receive?

_____
_____
_____
_____
_____
_____
_____
_____
_____
_____
_____
_____
_____
_____
_____
_____
_____

What was it like to listen from this place of ultimate loving?

_____
_____
_____
_____
_____
_____
_____
_____
_____
_____

Follow God's Guidance

As a life coach, I've discovered that only a small portion of people's challenges comes from not knowing what to do. The vast majority of their challenges come in doing what they know to do—in following through. So, in this place of deep connection with God, we can ask for and receive divine guidance. But this is just the beginning of our journey, isn't it?

Perhaps that is why I struggled for months to write this particular section on following God's direction. I believe this is because taking consistent action on His instructions has been (by far) the most challenging of the Sacred Six for me.

After several writing attempts, I finally received some extraordinary counsel. God said, "Let Me speak to them directly." Here's what came forward. If you are willing, I would ask now that you open your heart wide, step fully into your loving and read what follows as a communication directly from God to you:

Dear One,

I am here. I know you and love you completely, beyond your ability to comprehend. I always have and always will. Always. Under all circumstances. For all time and beyond all time. No matter what.

When you are in the experience of your loving—when you let go and surrender to My will—when you trust deep in your soul that I will provide for your needs— when you listen to me from your heart—you create a condition where I can speak to you directly. In this place, you can hear Me and receive My counsel.

Follow My guidance and I will take you to places you

could never otherwise discover. The plans you make always come from where you live on the Wisdom Curve and are therefore limited. The plans I reveal to you are not bound in any way.

Follow My guidance and you become unstuck in your life. Repeating negative patterns give way to new adventures, as I close old doors that need to be closed and open new doors that need to be opened.

Follow My guidance and I will take you to the desires of your soul. Not the desires of your ego, but your soul. As you pursue the yearnings I have placed in your heart, I will bring precisely the lessons needed to fulfill your divine destiny.

Follow My guidance and We will live in partnership. You will move beyond belief in a distant God, to a place where you carry Me in your heart moment by moment. You will live in the knowing that I am your one and only Source and that together, We are senior to any circumstance.

Follow My guidance and your life will work—and it will work brilliantly. Remember, there is no mountain on Earth that cannot be scaled six inches at a time and there is no challenge We cannot face together. Remember who you have as a partner.

Follow My guidance and know there is always a gift in the challenge greater than the challenge itself or I wouldn't bring it to you. In this way, I bring to you only that which is good.

Here are some keys that will help you on Our journey.

Stay connected to Me. Create special time in the stillness for us to commune regularly. Just you and Me. Do what feeds our relationship. Go to a nonjudgmental place of worship, or walk in nature, or meditate, or journal or be with My animals, or read sacred texts. Do what connects Us in your heart and do it often.

Learn to manage your thinking and speaking. This is the essence of faith, the faith required especially when you experience life as difficult. This will anchor you in the truth of Our being and will carry you to heights you cannot now imagine.

Create a system of loving, supportive community. Be with people who know Me and believe in you. Find people who are on your path and share specific promises to take specific action. Do this over and over, eliminating one challenge after another. Bring forth the desires of your heart, evolving as you go.

Remember, I do not promise comfort that ultimately lacks fulfillment. I bring you fulfillment that ultimately offers comfort.

I love you and I am here for you—forever.

– God

Wow! He gets right to the point, doesn't He?

Consider the possibility that we are so loved that we are given an entire physical Universe in which we get to express. This is the realm of doing. Here is where we get to jump in the pool, to play, to take action, to discover, to grow and to launch the journey of our life work—to create with unmolded clay. Here's where our spirituality gets honed in the real world.

Bottom line: when we love, surrender and trust, we can hear His guidance. The next step is simply to follow orders, to do what He says. In following His counsel, life just plain works and, as He says, "it will work brilliantly." And this is true even when His guidance appears at first as difficult or impossible.

As I shared, for me, obeying God has been far easier said than done. The very notion of being obedient to anything or anyone can make the hairs stand up on the back of my neck. It brings to mind images of servitude, dominance and oppression. But I've come to learn that my automatic ego-based reaction has nothing to do with why God invites us to follow His counsel.

Consider the possibility that God doesn't ask us to obey because He needs our compliance in any way. God asks us to follow His direction so we can lead a truly magnificent life. The more we listen from the heart and follow His direction, the more life works, the more effective and joyful we become, the more on track we are in fulfilling our highest destiny— however that may look.

When massive ships sail into port, the captain relinquishes control to a local port pilot who brings the craft safely into docking. This is done because there is no way the captain can know all the dangers and changing intricacies of every port.

Is it possible that in the same way, we are asked to follow instructions from One who knows the intricacies of our highest potential before we do? Is it possible that God is ever-present, totally available to guide us in our amazing process of evolving? Is it possible we are loved this much?

Consider the possibility that obedience to God isn't a burdensome obligation. It's an enormous love-based invitation that leads us to discoveries and experiences we could never choreograph on our own.

For Todd, an LCA seminar participant, life had been tough growing up in communist Hungary. For some reason, his mother always seemed to be easily irritated. She was an angry woman who yelled at him frequently for the smallest infractions.

Because of her sour attitude, Todd was reluctant to bring his friends home. In addition, he was embarrassed because she was missing fingers from an industrial accident.

When he was old enough, he ran away, snuck out from behind the Iron Curtain and made a good life for himself in the United States. Because of his past, he never called home.

In one of our follow-up courses, I challenged everyone to listen to their guidance and make a commitment to take action, even if that required stretching outside of their comfort zone. Participants began to share their commitments to finish a book, clean out their garage or pay off a debt.

At that point, Todd started to get angry. He stood up and said that none of those actions were real stretches. He had received strong inner guidance to call his mom, whom he hadn't spoken to in 20 years, and he promised to call her that week. Now that was a stretch!

It took some effort, but finally he was able to track down his mother. Then he called her. At first, she didn't believe it was him. She thought her son had been killed like so many others who tried to escape. When she realized she was speaking to

WHAT IF—

God doesn't ask us to obey because He needs our compliance in any way. God asks us to follow His direction so we can lead a truly magnificent life.

WHAT IF—

Obedience to God isn't a burdensome obligation. It's an enormous love-based invitation that leads us to discoveries and experiences we could never choreograph on our own.

her long-lost boy, she wept tears of joy from the unexpected reunion.

Before they hung up, she wanted Todd to know something she had never told him; something she could not risk keeping to herself should they not have another chance to speak with each other.

Before she married Todd's father, she was married to another man she loved dearly. During World War II, she and her husband were hiding Jews from the Nazis.

When their efforts were discovered, the Nazis burst into their home and shot her husband point blank. Then they demanded that she tell them where the Jews were. She told them she didn't know.

That was when they began removing her fingers, one at a time until she revealed their location. The Jews were then pulled from their hiding place and executed.

Todd's mother was so angry, so hurt, so filled with guilt that she took it out on her son in the years that followed. From the depths of her heart, she wanted Todd to know how sorry she was and asked for his forgiveness.

Shaken deeply, Todd now had a profound understanding of who his mother truly was. In an instant, decades of embarrassment and bitterness were replaced with an intense respect and compassion.

What would have been missing from Todd's life if he not had the courage to follow his guidance as uncomfortable as it was?

So here are three major insights I've gleaned over the years that have made following His guidance somewhat easier and more fulfilling. I hope they will be helpful to you as well.

Helpful Hint 1: Embrace Your Divine Curriculum.

I've heard it said that life is one of the few games where the objective is to figure out the instructions. Consider the possibility that the challenges you are currently facing in life are not there by accident. Consider the possibility that you and God have already co-created a life path that is totally unique to you.

Also, consider the possibility that when you identify your greatest internal and external challenges, you actually have clarified your own divine curriculum. This is the hand you have been dealt, the hand you have before you, and this is true even if you wish it weren't.

The good news is that in identifying your greatest challenges, you identify a big piece of life's instructions. You clarify the tasks and lessons that are absolutely perfect for moving you up the Wisdom Curve.

Let's do a quick exercise that might be very useful for you. Please stop right now and grab your pen. Seriously, this will be MUCH more powerful if you write down your answers rather than just thinking about them. And remember, your answers are for your eyes only, unless you choose to share them.

What are your five greatest *external* challenges?

Examples of external challenges include the areas of career, relationships, finances, incomplete tasks, living environment, health and family issues.

1 _____

2 _____

3 _____

4 _____

5 _____

What are your five greatest *internal* challenges?

Examples of internal challenges include fear, stress, anger, addictions, depression, guilt, resentment, procrastination, overwhelm, hurt from the past and self-judgment.

1. _____

2. _____

3. _____

4. _____

5. _____

Now consider the possibility that what we create on the outside begins with what we create on the inside. What we produce externally (like the quality of our relationships, the effectiveness in our careers, the numbers on our financial statement) is determined by the qualities of our internal ways of being (like integrity, confidence, vision and tenacity). Does this resonate as true for you?

Imagine for a moment that the external and internal challenges you just listed above, were projected on a giant movie screen. Like this:

WHAT IF—

*Life is one of the few games where the objective
is to figure out the instructions.*

WHAT IF—

*When you identify your greatest internal and
external challenges, you actually clarify
your own divine curriculum.*

WHAT IF—

*What we create on the outside begins with
what we create on the inside.*

Healing From the Inside Out

Consider the possibility that all of our external and internal challenges are creations that come from somewhere. Just like a projector sends an image to a screen, in the same way, we unconsciously project the challenges we are facing into our lives.

Once we clarify our internal and external challenges, the next opportunity is to discover what we are doing to manifest these challenges. In other words, we shift our focus from the screen to the projector. This is a major step in eliminating the source of destructive patterns that have been showing up over and over again.

I'm not saying that we are directly responsible for creating every personal tragedy. There may be nothing a parent could have done to prevent the death of a child. A community is not at fault for the hurricane that destroyed it.

What I am saying is that there is great value in exploring our inner roles that manifest in external outcomes. Here is an example.

A former NFL linebacker, Earnest stood six-foot five, weighing a good 280 pounds. He was hurting tremendously and utterly despondent. After losing his carpet cleaning business, the woman of his dreams left for parts unknown.

Because of his raging, his adult children weren't speaking to him and he'd just been diagnosed with stage two pancreatic cancer.

In our early sessions, Earnest's focus was entirely on how the people in his life had let him down. He was 100 percent focused on the screen and 0 percent focused on how he was projecting these consequences into his own life.

WHAT IF—

*All of our external and internal challenges are
creations that come from somewhere. Just like a
projector sends an image to a screen, in the same way,
we unconsciously project the challenges
we are facing into our lives.*

Have you ever experienced a similar place of hurting; your own dark night of the soul? When we feel most oppressed by life circumstances, it can be quite difficult to see any good coming from the challenge or to feel God's loving presence. Yet this is precisely the instant when we are most invited to expand. And when the pain is intense enough, this can become the tipping point where we become humbled and open to spiritual counsel.

In our third session, Earnest had a major discovery; there was something in common with every one of the challenges on his screen. Fundamental to each one, was something we call a "core issue"—an underlying, intense self-judgment created in childhood. This was his projector.

First for Earnest, there was a deep sense of being "not good enough." Second, he had a belief that he was fundamentally "weak." Third, he believed he "wasn't worth loving." All three were instilled in childhood by an angry, workaholic father. Intellectually, Earnest knew that none of these core issues were even close to being true. Yet, because emotions are not bound by truth or logic, his core issues persisted in full force.

Earnest continued on to discover that behind each of these core issues was a world of hurt. But because he had been taught "Quit your crying! Grow up! Don't be such a wimp! Be a man!" Earnest learned in no uncertain terms, that it wasn't OK for him to experience these emotions.

Just like Emily, if Earnest couldn't experience his hurt, there was no way he could heal his emotional pain. As a result, his core issues continued on, powerfully projecting a long list of challenges onto the screen of his life.

For decades he'd been driven to avoid the pain of these core issues. He did this by trying to gather all the external evidence that his internal core issues were not true—an exhaustive, abusive and impossible task.

In his efforts to avoid the hurt of "not good enough," he was driven to be in control and to perfectionism. In his efforts to avoid the hurt in "weak," he was driven to be tough and mean. In his efforts to avoid the hurt of "not worth loving" he was driven to be liked and respected. And in his attachment to be honored by others, he pushed people away, including his own family.

Once Earnest became aware of his core issues and how they played out, he became willing to let go, to surrender his hurt, literally redefining what it means to be courageous.

Witnessing this big man giving up having to be the tough guy, releasing a lifetime of pain, heaving tears, groping for tissues—was a profoundly liberating and moving experience for both of us.

For Earnest, the insights he gleaned resulted in a monumental shift in his behavior. Instead of feeling victimized by life's circumstances, he came to realize that his list of challenges where brought to him so he could heal his core issues.

He discovered that every challenge he was facing pointed to a core self-judgment in dire need of healing. In that instant, Earnest had the profound realization that God had never been against him. God had simply been bringing lessons so the insanely hurtful lies Earnest had perpetrated against himself could be healed on the deepest level.

He then moved to a whole new dimension of personal responsibility, powerfully shifting his focus from blaming to healing. In discovering, embracing and mastering his divine curriculum, he shifted from being the victim to being the victor.

Over time and with solid support, he continued to listen and follow God's guidance, taking right action. He healed his core issues in the LCA Weekend seminar and addressed each of his challenges in our follow-up course. Earnest restored his health and went on to become the dad his kids always wanted to love and respect.

For more guidance on how to identify and heal core issues, read Bill Ferguson's book, '*Get Your Power Back.*'

http://www.masteryoflife.com/power.html

To learn more about the LCA Weekend and 7 Week Course, click here:

http://lcaproject.com/lcaweekend7weekcourse.html

Here is another even more personal example of how God can elevate us to a new level of consciousness. I recall a time in my own life when I was going through bankruptcy, foreclosure, tax issues and losing my wife and daughter through divorce. I had to let go of my family, business, reputation and possessions (including my '59 Jag). In my own dark night of my soul, I felt like God was reaching in, yanking my heart right out of my chest. The overwhelm was intense. The pain was excruciating. Do you know this kind of hurting?

Slowly, I began to dig my way out, but not from the same level of awareness that got me into such a mess in the first place. I had been shaken to a place of awakening. I was humbled; now hungry to learn what I had done to create such suffering, where before I had little interest.

In my openness to follow God's guidance, I was blessed with unexpected resources: tremendous support from my family, a short term job that required little energy from me and paid

WHAT IF—

God has simply been bringing lessons so the
insanely hurtful lies we have perpetrated
against ourselves can be healed
on the deepest level.

well, true friends who loved me unconditionally. The end result was my embrace of clear, essential life lessons vital to my evolution.

Now I see that this extremely difficult time is what it took to get my attention, to awaken me to a higher way of being. Although I wouldn't wish these lessons on anyone, in hindsight, I see it was a perfect part of my life curriculum.

I learned to be the kind of man a woman can love and respect. I learned on an experiential level that God is Source, not money. I learned that I'm not what I own or what other people think of me. I learned that God never walks away, even when I do. I learned that I don't have to be the Lone Ranger—that I grow best in a supportive community. I learned that my life is most fulfilled in my service to others.

Through tragedy, I was nudged a little bit up the Wisdom Curve. About six months later, I looked back and every one of those challenges had been resolved through right action. In fact, it was this experience that inspired me to change careers from real estate to sharing the possibilities of life through coaching, writing and leading seminars. I redefined my dreams, becoming an even better version of myself.

Consider the possibility that with unimaginable love, God has created for us this stunning physical utopia we call Earth. The primary purpose of this breathtaking physical domain is to provide a home for us to evolve as beings, to thrive, to prosper —to be beneficial stewards for one another and our planet.

Consider the possibility that God loves us so much that in following His guidance, we are each directed to our own unique destiny—the path that ultimately brings us the most fulfilment. Initially, this path may not take us where we thought our

WHAT IF—

*With unimaginable love, God has created for
us this stunning physical utopia we call Earth.
The primary purpose of this breathtaking physical
domain is to provide a home for us to evolve as beings,
to thrive, to prosper—to be beneficial stewards for one
another and our planet.*

greatest joy would reside. But in our love, surrender, trust and listening—we will be guided to our highest divine expression.

Consider the possibility that in this very moment, life is exactly the way it is supposed to be—that we have just the right challenges and just the right resources, even if it doesn't feel that way.

As we awaken in our awareness, our immediate opportunity is to free up the energy formerly consumed by denial, blaming, compensating and resisting. We then move to a place of accepting and addressing what is.

In partnership with God, we are invited to face our greatest issues head on, generating the commitment to follow His guidance, doing whatever it takes to master these challenges. We claim full responsibility and in accepting the invitation, become fully engaged in cleaning up our lives one day at a time.

Whatever our list of challenges, no matter how severe, they are brought to us as a gift of learning and healing. They are our unique set of lessons, the mastery of which will grow us up the Wisdom Curve in the most miraculous ways. And as odd as it may seem, ultimately, they are brought with great love from a Creator who knows who we are capable of becoming.

As we master our challenges, the tremendous energy they consumed is liberated. Then our opportunity is to channel all that freed-up voltage into manifesting the dreams of our heart. What an exciting turning point!

Manifesting Our Dreams

Jack Canfield shares about Monty, the son of an itinerant horse trainer. The boy's family would go from ranch to ranch

WHAT IF—

In this very moment, life is exactly the way it is supposed to be—that we have just the right challenges and just the right resources, even if it doesn't feel that way.

WHAT IF—

In partnership with God, we are invited to face our greatest issues head on, generating the commitment to follow His guidance, doing whatever it takes to master these challenges.

training horses. As a result, his high school education was continually interrupted. When he was a senior, he was asked to write a paper about what he wanted to be and do when he grew up.

That night he wrote a seven-page paper describing his goal of someday owning a horse ranch. He wrote about his dream in great detail and he even drew a diagram of a 200-acre ranch, showing the location of all the buildings, the stables and track. Then he drew a detailed floorplan for a 4,000 square-foot house that would sit on his dream ranch.

The next day he handed it in to his teacher. Two days later, he received his paper back. On the front page was a large red "F" with a note that read, "See me after class." Later that day, the boy did as instructed and asked why she gave him an "F" on his paper.

The teacher said, "This is an unrealistic dream for a boy like you. You come from an itinerant family. You have no resources. Owning a horse ranch requires a lot of money. You have to pay for the land, the materials, the breeding stock and stud fees. There's no way you could ever do it. Then the teacher added, "Here's your paper. If you will rewrite it with a more realistic goal, I will reconsider your grade."

Monty went home and thought about his challenge long and hard. A week later, the boy handed the same paper making no changes at all. He said to the teacher, "You can keep your "F" and I will keep my dream."

Decades later, a wealthy rancher shared his story with an elementary school group assembled in his home. Accompanying the children was an older wiser woman, the very teacher who tried to limit a young boy's dream.

Monty shared with the kids, "You are now sitting in my 4,000 square-foot house in the middle of my 200 acre horse ranch. See that document framed over the fireplace? It's that same paper I wrote as a boy, complete with its big red "F."

In 1998 Robert Redford co-produced and acted in a movie about Monty's uncanny ability to work with troubled horses. The movie was titled, "The Horse Whisperer."

Consider the possibility that just as God brings us specific challenges to grow us up the Wisdom Curve, he also plants deep desires in us to achieve certain lifetime goals: to find a wonderful partner and start a family, to own a successful business, to heal abused animals, to live in a 4,000 square-foot home on a 200-acre horse ranch. What lessons do you think Monty learned as he achieved the very thing he was told he couldn't do?

What is a dream of your heart, the manifestation of which might bring you both great satisfaction and the perfect lessons required to evolve as a being?

We can either embrace our challenges or resist them. We can go after our dreams or have them languish in the realm of "someday." When we resist our challenges, the lessons tend to repeat and amplify. When we ignore the dreams of our heart, a part of us begins to die inside.

In surrendering to the tasks that lie before us, we open ourselves to sacred guidance and the journey of transformation begins. So, are you willing to discover, embrace and master your own divine curriculum? And are you willing to listen and to follow divine guidance as you fully engage your challenges and manifest the dreams of your heart?

Helpful Hint 2: Mastering This Thing Called "Attitude."

In our efforts to follow divine guidance, comes both the opportunity and duty, as God said, to "manage our thinking and speaking." We all know the importance of attitude. A lousy attitude produces lousy results. A great attitude carries us through tough times, escorting us on to our higher aspirations.

Most of us learned about attitude in childhood. I'll bet I'm not the only one who heard these words growing up, "You can come out of your room when you do something about that attitude!"

So we go to our room and somehow we're supposed to figure out how to change our mental/emotional state. We have been told to manage attitude, but how many of us have been shown HOW?

The 3 Mind Factors

My dear friend, Stephen Vannoy, wrote a remarkable, best-selling parenting/leadership book entitled, "The 10 Greatest Gifts I Give My Children." In it he describes the 3 Mind Factors, the Energy Circle and the power of Forward Focused Questions. For me, these concepts have been by far the best answer to the question, "HOW does one manage attitude?"

Here is an adapted explanation of Steve's concepts that have really helped me live the Sacred Six. Let's begin with:

WHAT IF—

Just as God brings us specific challenges to grow us up the Wisdom Curve, he also plants deep desires in us to achieve certain lifetime goals.

WHAT IF—

Are you willing to discover, embrace and master your own divine curriculum? And are you willing to listen and to follow divine guidance as you fully engage your challenges and manifest the dreams of your heart?

WHAT IF—

You can come out of your room when you do something about that attitude!

The 3 Mind Factors:

1. The mind can only focus on one thing at a time.

2. The mind creates in the direction of its focus.

3. The mind triggers on questions.

The first mind factor reveals that at any given moment, our conscious mind can only focus on one thing at a time. At first, I didn't believe this to be true because I am a fairly accomplished multi-tasker. Then one day I noticed someone texting and driving. At any given instant, their conscious focus was either on texting OR what was happening on the road—but not both at the same instant.

Dr. Joseph Dispenza says the human brain processes at the rate of 400 billion bits of information per second. Amazing! Yet, I've discovered that at any given instant, I can only consciously focus on one thing at a time.

This realization is important because if our focus is on what's going well, we CAN'T be focused on how difficult and terrible life is. If we're focused on what we appreciate about someone, we CAN'T be focused on what we dislike about that person. If we're stoking the furnace of self-esteem, we can't be dwelling on the awfulness of our own shortcomings.

The second mind factor reveals that whatever we focus on tends to expand. This principle can work for us or against us. If we focus on what's going well, life appears to be going our way. If we focus on how little time we have, we create stress and overwhelm. If we focus on what we appreciate about a colleague, that relationship tends to improve. If we focus on our lack, we create more lack. And in counting blessings, we actually expand our experience of prosperity.

WHAT IF—

The 3 Mind Factors are:

1. The mind can only focus on one thing at a time.
2. The mind creates in the direction of its focus.
3. The mind triggers on questions.

The third mind factor is well-known by effective parents, educators and business leaders. The instant we ask someone (or even ourselves) a question, something magical happens. Like a knee jerk reaction, the listener's mind switches into search mode in an effort to find the answer.

To demonstrate this point in seminars, I will often ask the audience how much time we have left together. As if on que, everyone instantly looks at their watch, phone or the clock on the wall, at which point I ask them, "What just happened?"

What they quickly realize is that their response to a question is nothing less than automatic. They also discover how this insight can be applied powerfully in daily communications.

By asking questions strategically, we can serve the people around us by directing their awareness. What are you grateful for? What are your strengths? Where have you been successful in the past? How can you apply your past experience to solving this current challenge?

The Energy Circle

Now let's add something we call the Energy Circle, to the 3 Mind Factors and see what happens.

Imagine for a moment, that the circle below represents your life. In this circle is everything that has meaning to you: your health, your values, your family, your career, your finances, your possessions, your spirituality.

The Energy Circle

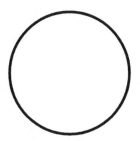

Could it be said that each of us has a common asset called 24-hours a day? Could it also be said that our success in life is determined to a great degree, by the quality of the decisions we make, one 24-hour period after another?

If we make enough bad decisions over time, we find ourselves on the street corner with a piece of cardboard that says, "God Bless. Anything Helps." If we make enough great decisions, we are creating our own non-profit organization to help those in need.

So let's take a look at some of these decisions we make over time.

Imagine that this Energy Circle has a front side and a back side. On the back side of the Energy Circle is "What's not working?" If the mind can only focus on one thing at a time, and I'm focused on "What's not working?" what am I NOT focused on? That's right, "What is working?" So let's put "What's not working?" on the back side and "What is working?" on the front side like this:

The Energy Circle

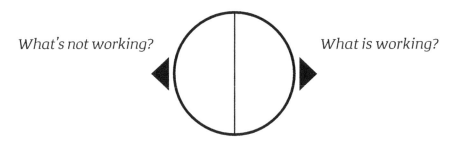

What's not working?   *What is working?*

Now, imagine for a moment that you come home after a really tough day. You have about four hours between the moment you walk in the front door and the moment your head hits the pillow. What is the impact on your family if you spend two of those four hours on the back side of the Energy Circle complaining about all the things that didn't work that day? Does that complaining help or hurt your loved ones? And once those two hours are spent, can you ever get those two hours back?

The cost is enormous, however, the greatest impact of living on the back side of the Energy circle isn't the loss of those two hours. An even greater cost is that we have the power to bring our whole family into that place of negativity—the back side of the Energy Circle.

If this happens on a daily basis, how excited is your family going to be when they hear you walking through the front door? And if your children need some advice that evening, how likely are they to seek it from you if you are living in this state of unapproachability?

What might be the result if we left our challenges at the office and deliberately came home WAY on the front side of the Energy Circle?

Here's another perspective. On the back side of the Energy Circle, I can be focused on "Why are things so difficult?" On the front side, "How do I get so much done so easily?"

The Energy Circle

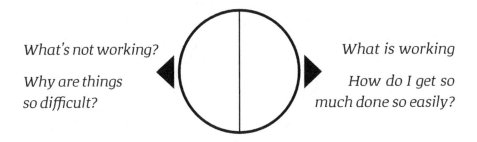

What's not working?

Why are things so difficult?

What is working

How do I get so much done so easily?

Consider the possibility that what creates overwhelm and stress isn't so much the circumstances in life, but how we relate to those circumstances. In other words, we literally <u>create</u> anxiety by positioning our challenges on the back side of the Energy Circle.

Brian Tracy shares how some folks live in the mantra, "I have to—but I can't! I have to—but I can't!!" Other people live in the question, "Why do things always take so much time?" Or "Why am I so slow?" Or "Why are things so difficult?" Is it possible that engaging in that kind of backward focused questioning dramatically influences both our reality and our outcomes?

Of course, the really great news is, we have a choice about this. What difference will it make as you ask yourself questions from the front side of the Energy Circle? "Why do things always seem to go my way?" Or "How do I get so much done so easily?" Or, as brother Bill has been known to say, "Why is the grass always greener on MY side of the fence?"

Let's look at relationships. On the back side: "What is it I don't like about _____?" In the blank, insert anybody's name. And on the front side: "What do I appreciate about _____?" and insert the same name.

The Energy Circle

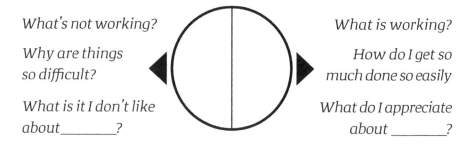

What's not working?

Why are things so difficult?

What is it I don't like about _____?

What is working?

How do I get so much done so easily

What do I appreciate about _____?

Years ago, I was married to wonderful woman whose daughter was just entering her teens. I recall a two-week time period where it seemed that everything I asked my step-daughter to do was met with intense resistance. Her room looked like a tornado in a bad mood and her bathroom looked like a cosmetic explosion.

She promised to clean both her room and the bathroom by the end of the day, after which nothing had changed in the slightest. Then I'd get a barrage of excuses, none of which was substantial.

By the end of those two weeks, I was ready to pull my hair out! At one point, I was so angry that I had to remove myself from the house. As I stomped across a nearby field, I ranted about how unfair life is that I had to deal with such an obnoxious, uncooperative brat!

Then something shifted. I began to recall my teachings to others, particularly, the 3 Mind Factors and Energy Circle. Then it hit me hard. I'd been holding my stepdaughter on the back side of the Energy Circle for weeks. I'd been entirely focused on what she was doing wrong—what I didn't like about her and boy, was I creating in the direction of my focus!

In that instant, out in that field, I was humbled to tears. I shifted my attention to what was great about her—her creativity, how she made us all laugh, her incredible strength of character, her sense of justice, her generosity. I saw that God was bringing me a lesson. I was the one who first needed to change!

What blew me away was how quickly my outer circumstances changed when I created this internal shift. The instant I walked back into the house, she ran up to me, wrapped me in her arms and hugged me hard. Is it true that what we create on the outside begins with what we create on the inside?

Did her room and bath get cleaned up instantly? No. But the more I stayed on the front side, the more I responded rather than reacted. When I was on the front side, I was at peace and our cooperation moved to a much higher level. It took a little longer, but with time she became neater and more organized by her own choice.

How do these tools work in the realm of self-esteem? On the back side of the Energy Circle is: "What is it I don't like about myself?" On the front side is: "What I appreciate about myself."

The Energy Circle

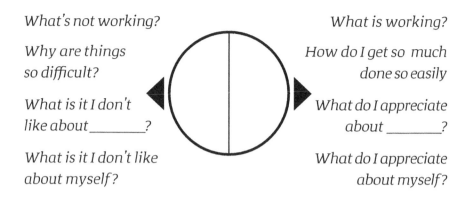

What's not working?

Why are things
so difficult?

What is it I don't
like about_____?

What is it I don't like
about myself?

What is working?

How do I get so much
done so easily

What do I appreciate
about _____?

What do I appreciate
about myself?

Earlier I shared the notion that each of us has a relationship with self—that there is a way that we speak to and treat ourselves. The quality of this relationship affects every aspect of life, which is why we are commanded to love self and others with everything we've got.

Yet in our culture, on which side of the Energy Circle do we have the most permission to hang out when it comes to how we regard ourselves?

It seems to me that all too often in our relationship with others, it's fine to put ourselves down, complain and speak negatively about our capabilities. That way no one feels threatened. But what would happen if one day you showed up at work incredibly enthusiastic for no reason? What would happen if you were thrilled about your own strengths and abilities, absolutely jazzed about how you planned to contribute to the organization? What would your colleagues think? How would you be judged? Can you see how living on the front side might be a little bit dangerous?

So if being on the front side of the Energy Circle about your-self can be threatening, and the mind can only focus on one thing at a time, what's the remaining alternative? Could this explain why so many people hang out on the back side, strug-gling in their efforts to maintain self-confidence?

Perhaps this is why living a great life is not for the weak of heart. It can take some real courage to live splendidly can't it? As Marianne Williamson states so eloquently, "Our deepest fear is not that we are inadequate. Our deepest fear is that we are powerful beyond measure. It is our Light, not our Dark-ness, that most frightens us."

Life on the back side, is a formula for failure, a roadmap to misery. It destroys the experience of loving and our quality of life. It's living on the non-love side of the gate, separating us from experiencing God's caring. In this place, people can feel disconnected, lost and they do weird things.

On the back side, people feel dominated by their circum-stances and have little interest following His guidance. Living in this painful state makes doing His will incredibly difficult and just isn't all that much fun.

Life on the front side is just the opposite. It makes following God's guidance dramatically more appealing. And here's the main point—we get to decide which half of the Energy Circle we call home. Truly, it is a choice; a choice we get to make moment by moment.

The Immense Power of Forward Focused Questions

But how do we do this? When we become aware that we're on the back side, how do we actually shift to the front side? The secret lies in the third mind factor.

The mind triggers on questions.

The key to living on the front side of the Energy Circle is to ask yourself and others what we call a "Forward Focused Question." A "Backward Focused Question" pulls people to the back side. A Forward Focused Question pulls people to the front side.

My dad was a master at Backward Focused Questions. "Why did it take you so long?" "What were you thinking?" "Why didn't you listen to me?" "Why didn't you do it right the first time?"

He didn't ask these questions to hurt me. I know he had the best intentions. What he didn't realize, however, was that Randy's little brain was left with, 'What is the matter with me?' and 'Why can't I do anything right?'

Because the mind triggers on questions, there is never a lack of answers. Forward-Focused Questions build the self-esteem that excellence demands, while Backward Focused Questions destroy it.

Unconsciously, dad was chopping me off at the knees and expecting me to run a marathon. It didn't work very well. Later in life, to his immense credit, he saw what he was doing and consciously worked to turn things around. Yea Dad!

Asking Forward Focused Questions, builds people and builds relationships. It triggers people's minds to the front side. When an individual, a family member or team is on the front side of the Energy Circle, great things happen. People take responsibility. They become more resourceful, more effective and just plain happier.

I wish you could be in the front of the room with me when I teach culture-building leadership skills to organizations.

WHAT IF—

*If being on the front side of the Energy Circle
about yourself can be threatening, and
the mind can only focus on one thing at a time,
what's the remaining alternative?
Could this explain why so many people hang out
on the back side, struggling in their efforts to
maintain self-confidence?*

WHAT IF—

*The key to living on the front side of the Energy Circle
is to ask yourself and others a "Forward Focused
Question." "A Backward Focused Question" pulls people
to the back side. A Forward Focused Question pulls
people to the front side.*

You would see people's faces light up as they get on the front side of the Energy Circle and realize that every single team member has the power to impact the well-being of the entire organization.

Here's another key point: when you ask yourself a Forward Focused Question, your mind is directed to the front side as well. Sounds crazy but when you are feeling down, asking and answering Forward Focused Questions can restore you to being in a great frame of mind. Here are some examples that might be useful.

Forward Focused Questions for building self-esteem include:

What am I doing well?

What are some of my greatest attributes?

How have I overcome obstacles in the past and what did I learn?

In what ways have I been a great mom, dad or friend?

What are some of my most significant blessings?

Forward Focused Questions for building others are:

What achievements from the past are you most proud of?

What are some of your greatest qualities?

How did you come up with such a brilliant idea?

How did you get that done so quickly?

What are some of your thoughts on this?

WHAT IF—

When you ask yourself a Forward Focused Question, your mind is directed to the front side. Sounds crazy but when you are feeling down, asking and answering Forward Focused Questions can restore you to being in a great frame of mind.

For an expanded list of Forward Focused Questions, go to:

www.lcaproject.com/the-opening-videos

What are some additional Forward Focused Questions that might be especially useful for where you are in your life right now?

Forward Focused Questions for yourself:

_____

_____

_____

_____

_____

_____

_____

Forward Focused Questions for others:

_____

_____

_____

_____

_____

_____

_____

We can operate from the front side or the back side about ANYTHING! Take any of the challenges you are currently facing and notice that in every case, you can hold that challenge on either side of the Energy Circle. Is this also true about your dreams? Is it true about most everything?

Also, you can come up with real evidence to prove the validity of the back side or the front side. In other words, whichever side of the Energy Circle you're on—YOUR RIGHT! I could have easily taken pictures of my stepdaughter's bedroom and bath as evidence for what a rotten kid she was. But just as easily, couldn't I have built a case for her magnificence?

Perhaps what matters most isn't which side of the Energy Circle is right. Perhaps what matters most is which side works the best. So, on which side of the Energy Circle do you plan on taking up residence?

By the way, God doesn't expect us to live on the front side of the Energy Circle all the time. I don't know a single human who lives in this positive place constantly. I sure don't. The expectation is to be aware when we are on the back side, then to shift to the front side as quickly as possible. This, we can do. The more we practice using this tool, the stronger we become. And each day we are given a fresh opportunity to create anew. How great is that?

In managing my attitude—in living on the front side of the Energy circle—I create a state of consciousness that inspires my loving, helps me to surrender, anchors my trusting, facilitates my listening and empowers me to follow God's guidance. In this resourceful place, I have that feeling of being divinely on course, regardless of the challenges at hand. In this place, I am joyful, productive and at peace.

Many years ago, before I knew much about managing attitude, Steve Vannoy asked me to come over to go for a hike. I replied that I was having a tough day, that things weren't working well and that I didn't have the time.

Steve said, "Randy, you're not being effective anyway so why not come on over?" I couldn't argue with that logic so I got up from my desk and grabbed my hiking boots.

Steve knew I was feeling down, so at the trailhead he began asking me a series of forward focused questions. "Randy, how do you manage to move people through their challenges so fast? Randy, how did you connect with your audience to receive that standing ovation? Randy, what can you teach me about being an even better dad? Randy, what are you looking forward to as you serve even more people?" On and on he went. One forward focused question after another.

By the time we returned, I was higher than a kite! My self-confidence was soaring. That's when I said, "Dang, Steve! You are so lucky to have a friend like me who's always so positive!"

He just looked at me and grinned.

Helpful Hint 3: Manage the Body

I noticed a while back that I could be sailing along, following God's guidance on the front side of the energy circle, when in a heartbeat, I'd be yanked to the back side in a state of upset. Has this ever happened to you?

In an instant, I'd shift from riding the wave of life to being mauled by it. After this happened a few dozen times, I began to ask, "Why?" What was I missing that made this backslide possible? What was the lesson God was trying to teach me?

The answer that ensued has become the preventative maintenance piece that minimizes tough times when they hit. It's how caring for the physical body impacts the mind, the emotions and our spirituality. The first insight had to do with what I was putting into my body.

You need to know that I have always had a love affair with sugar. There's a part of me that could walk into a bakery and gobble down their entire inventory. No kidding! Just in

WHAT IF—

*Whatever side of the energy circle
you are on—you are right!
So perhaps what matters most isn't which
side of the Energy Circle is right. Maybe what
matters most is which side works the best.
On which side of the Energy Circle
do you plan on taking up residence?*

WHAT IF—

*The expectation is to be aware when we are on the
back side, then to shift to the front side as quickly
as possible. This, we can do. The more we practice
using, this tool, the stronger we become.
And each day we are given a fresh opportunity
to create anew. How great is that?*

writing about sweets, I salivate. But over time, I discovered an undeniable pattern. When I consumed certain kinds of sugar, in a matter of minutes, I'd become irritable, anxious and very negative in my thinking. In the span of a few minutes, I'd be treading water on the back side of the Energy Circle, feeling distant from my Maker.

Dr. Jennifer Bahr states that refined sugar releases inflammatory messengers called cytokines, which have been strongly associated with depression. And as nutritionists know all too well, the body's reaction after eating refined sugar is to produce excessive insulin to handle all the sweet stuff. Blood glucose then takes a nosedive which tells the adrenaline glands to get busy, which in turn causes irritability and anxiety. Yuck!

In addition, sugar compromises the immune system and robs us of vital nutrients. AND it's literally addictive, releasing opioids and dopamine. So, just as with narcotics, we end up craving a substance that damages the body, sabotages attitude and disconnects us from the experience of loving. The more we consume, the more we want and the worse it gets.

Randy's sweet tooth really didn't really like hearing all of this. And I've had to learn this lesson the hard way many, many times before I really got it for myself and many others:

Sugar = Pain!

More bad news. Sugar is in alcohol. I hate that! Excessive carbs turn into sugar. I hate that, too. But it's the way it is, isn't it?

There are so many good books on diet out there. This isn't one of them. The point I want to make is that what we put into the body, impacts our ability to live the Sacred Six. And as crazy

WHAT IF—

Sugar = Pain!

as it sounds, diet impacts our ability to relate with God.

At this point in my life, I seem to manage my consumption in a way that frees me from being pulled too far to the back side for any extended length of time. Ultimately, saying no to the dessert tray is a very small price to pay for the enormous number of benefits that come from living effectively and joyfully.

A second major insight in the body/spirit connection has to do with—you guessed it—exercise. Study after study correlates the relationship between our physiological and psychological optimum states. We know that exercise-induced endorphins bolster self-esteem, quality of sleep, memory, brain function, resilience and personal energy.

What many people don't know is that exercise makes a significant impact on our spirituality. Elevating our heart rate even for a short time dramatically impacts attitude which dramatically impacts our ability to follow God's guidance. Lethargy does the opposite. Does this resonate for you in your experience?

The good news is you don't have to be a decathlon athlete to reap these benefits. Begin with some enjoyment walks. Then consider slowly increasing your pace and distance, treasuring the gifts that surround you.

One of my favorite words in the English language is "alacrity." It means "cheerful briskness." When I walk at a fast pace, deliberately asking and answering questions that pull me to the front side of the energy circle, I'm consciously creating alacrity. I'm combining the body and the mind to generate the soul-centered energy required to follow God's counsel.

WHAT IF—

Exercise induced endorphins bolster self-esteem, quality of sleep, memory and brain function, resilience and personal energy.
What many people don't know is that exercise makes a significant impact on our spirituality.

Not only does it feel fantastic, it's revving my engine for a great day, psyching myself up for whatever God asks of me.

What happens when people love, surrender, trust, listen and follow their guidance?

The following story is from PropelSteps.com.

> *The year was 1892. The location was Stanford University.*
>
> *An 18-year-old student was struggling to pay his fees. He was an orphan, and not knowing where to turn for money, he came up with a bright idea. He and a friend decided to host a musical concert on campus to raise money for their education.*
>
> *They reached out to the great pianist Ignacy J. Paderewski. His manager demanded a guaranteed fee of $2000 for the piano recital. A deal was struck and the boys began to work to make the concert a success.*
>
> *The big day arrived. But unfortunately, they had not managed to sell enough tickets. The total collection was only $1600. Disappointed, they went to Paderewski and explained their plight. They gave him the entire $1600, plus a check for the $400 balance and promised to honor the check at the soonest possible opportunity.*
>
> *"No," said Paderewski. "This is not acceptable." He tore up the check, and told the two boys, "Here's the $1600. Please deduct whatever expenses you have incurred. Keep the money you need for your fees. And just give me whatever is left." The boys were surprised, and thanked him profusely.*

Is it possible when those boys fell short of funds that Paderewski tapped into divine guidance? Is it possible because of this man's love and compassion for the plight of others, he surrendered any attachment to the funds and trusted that all would be well? Is it possible that in that moment he listened and was instantly guided to right action?

The story continues.

> Paderewski later went on to become the Prime Minister of Poland. He was a great leader, but unfortunately when World War I began, Poland was ravaged. There were more than 1.5 million people starving in his country, and no money to feed them. Paderewski did not know where to turn for help so he reached out to the US Food and Relief Administration.
>
> The director was a man named Herbert Hoover — who later went on to become the U.S. President. Hoover agreed to help and quickly shipped tons of food grains to feed the starving Polish people.

HOOVER   PADEREWSKI

A calamity was averted. Paderewski was immensely relieved. He decided to meet with Hoover to express his gratitude personally. When Paderewski began to thank this man for his noble gesture, Hoover quickly interjected and said, "You shouldn't be thanking me Mr. Prime Minister. You may not remember this, but several years ago, you helped two young students go through college. I was one of them."

So just for fun, imagine it's a year from today:

- In your enhanced ability to love God, yourself and others—your quality of life is soaring.

- In your beautiful surrendering and trusting, you feel free and at peace, closer to God than ever before.

- In your heart-centered listening, you receive ongoing divine direction and a continual knowing that your life is on track.

- In identifying and embracing your challenges and dreams, your divine curriculum is crystal clear.

- In managing your attitude, you are joyful most of the time and far more effective, living WAY on the front side of the Energy Circle.

- In caring for your body, your highs last longer and your lows become less frequent. You bring alacrity to your life in your body/mind/emotion/spirit connection.

- In this heightened, resourceful state of awareness, you are following God's guidance, conquering one challenge after another, evolving up the Wisdom Curve, achieving the dreams of your heart.

Now here's a forward focused question just for you.

What does it feel like to live in this level of partnership with your Creator as you navigate through this amazing gift called, "life?"

_____
_____
_____
_____
_____
_____
_____
_____
_____
_____
_____
_____
_____
_____
_____
_____
_____
_____
_____
_____
_____
_____

Try It Out Exercise: Follow Your Guidance

Warning: The following exercise is not for the faint of heart. It takes some courage to stand back and identify what's not working in your life and the dreams of your heart. The benefits though, are ENORMOUS! For some, it's like being lost in the forest and discovering a compass. Complete this exercise with all your heart and you will generate clarity, direction and sense of hope.

OK! This is your chance!

Step 1:

Create for yourself a quiet time and place where you will be uninterrupted. Light a candle and ask with all your heart to experience the loving presence and assistance of God in this exercise, feeling grateful for knowing your prayer is already answered.

Step 2:

If you prefer that I guide you through the steps, just go to the video titled: Follow Through on the website below.

www.lcaproject.com/the-opening-videos

Step 3:

There is such power in clarifying your challenges and dreams. Imagine that if you could just write them down, the challenges would vanish and your dreams would manifest.

Begin by detailing an expanded list of current challenges in your life, both internal and external. **Be sure and include the challenges you listed on page 140**. *Acknowledging them is the first step in regaining a sense of confident direction.*

As I shared, **external** challenges may include health, career, finances, relationships, living environment, family issues. My primary, specific, external challenges are:

_____

_____

_____

_____

_____

_____

_____

_____

_____

_____

Internal challenges may include fear, stress, addictions, anger, depression, guilt, resentment, procrastination, over-whelm, hurt from the past and self-judgment. My primary, specific, internal challenges are:

_____

_____

_____

_____

_____

_____

_____

_____

_____

Step 4:

Imagine for a moment that you have already succeeded in handling the challenges you've listed above. Really let in how good that feels! From this joyful place in consciousness, list your greatest **dreams**—*the dreams of your heart. This is what you would love to have, do, be or feel in your lifetime, even if you do not yet know how. Again, imagine that in detailing your dreams below, they would actually manifest in your life! These are the dreams of my heart:*

_____

_____

_____

_____

_____

_____

_____

_____

_____

_____

_____

_____

_____

_____

_____

_____

_____

_____

_____

_____

_____

_____

_____

_____

Step 5:

From a place of love, surrender and trust, create in yourself a willingness and commitment to move forward in your divine curriculum—to follow through on God's guidance— and ethically do whatever it takes to handle your challenges and move forward on your dreams.

If you truly do not know how to resolve a particular challenge, generate a passionate commitment to find out how. Seek the assistance from those who have demonstrated mastery in those areas. Every challenge and every dream has a pathway to its resolution or God would not have given it to you. The level of your intention is what brings solutions forward.

Sometimes in my seminars, I will ask people to raise their hands if they could come up with $50,000 in 48 hours if they had to. Then I ask if the life of the person you loved most, depended upon your coming up with $50,000 in 48 hours, who could come up with the money? Significantly more hands are raised in response to this second question.

What changed? Consider the possibility that we get to determine the intensity of our own commitment. And guess whose life is at stake? Maybe not your physical life, just the degree to which you are truly alive while you're alive.

A key to stoking the furnace of our own motivation is to let in the cost of not moving forward, then to let in the emotional benefits of victory. With respect to your greatest challenges and dreams, what would be the three greatest **costs** *of ignoring the action steps required to move forward?*

_____

_____

_____

_____

_____

_____

_____

_____

_____

_____

_____

_____

_____

*What will be the three greatest **benefits** of powerfully resolving your challenges and making your dreams real?*

_____

_____

_____

_____

_____

_____

_____

_____

_____

_____

The willingness to do creates the ability to do. What precedes a breakthrough is the willingness to face the issue at hand with intense determination. Are you truly willing, in partnership with God, to do whatever is required in taking constructive action?

_____

Step 6:

Now go inward. In a comfortable private setting, close your eyes and take some beautiful full breaths of life. Enjoy the experience of inhaling deeply into the area of your heart.

As you do, feel the sacred Presence. Once again feel and see the brilliant white light of God's Holy Spirit in the area of your heart. Feel this stunning radiance as it heals everything it illuminates. Feel your heart once again filled to overflowing with divine loving. Keep breathing into this area as God's light continues to expand, once again filling your entire body.

In this experience, all urgency and hurt just fall away. As you actually experience becoming this love—becoming this light—you feel ultimately safe and cared for. Feel the love. Feel the joy. Feel the alacrity and the oneness with God.

Step 7:

In this place of peace, this place of stillness—ask and listen. God, I let go and surrender. I embrace my divine curriculum. I'm willing to do whatever it takes, whatever you ask me to do. How do you want me to handle the challenges before me? How do you want me to address my dreams?

In your own words, just ask God for guidance now. Be still. Ask. And listen.

Great. Now, you may want to ask if there's anything else He wants to share with you. Then again, listen with all your heart.

Step 8:

When you're ready, prepare to come back in a state of joyful determination. Feel the seat beneath you. Gently move your body. And when you are ready, just open your eyes. Take a deep breath. And write down the guidance you received:

_____

_____

_____

_____

_____

_____

_____

_____

_____

_____

_____

_____

_____

_____

_____

_____

_____

_____

_____

_____

_____

_____

_____

_____

_____

_____

_____

_____

Step 9:

Are you willing to follow through on your guidance? What actions are you going to take and by when?

Step 10:

In this precious union with Spirit, take a moment just to say "thank you." Feel the gratitude of receiving insight and direction and express your appreciation.

THE SACRED SIX:

#5 - APPRECIATE AND CELEBRATE

Appreciate

I had no idea that morning the enormity of the gift I was being given. As I jotted down these six fundamental ways of being, I was literally inscribing what was to become the foundation of my life. And I certainly had no clue that I would be sharing these tenets with others. Yet as the words, "Appreciate and Celebrate" were etched onto my journal and into my heart, I was touched by the loving in His every word.

On some level, I'd always thought that joy was just a by-product of good living, something God tolerated as a result of my obedience. But in this fifth directive, I was being asked to deliberately savor the gift of life. It was only after years of contemplation that I got on the deepest level that God truly wants me to be joyful—and not just joyful, but outrageously joyful!

So here is a simple question from my heart to yours: Would you like to have more joy in your life? Not a fleeting gratification, but waves and waves of soul-filling joy? Consciously appreciating and celebrating seems to be the key. Strap on your seat belt because this fifth step is where quality of life really skyrockets.

What does it feel like to be in a state of appreciation?

Just for fun, right now, please write down the five beings or things you most appreciate in your life:

1 _____

2 _____

3 _____

4 _____

5 _____

What does it feel like just focusing on what you appreciate? Did you feel your spirit lift a bit? Let's take it a step deeper.

Just for a moment, think of someone who's most dear to you. Now, what would happen to your level of appreciation if you knew this person had one week to live? Wouldn't you treasure them tremendously? What would happen if you were the one with a single week left to go? Wouldn't you cherish this gift of life and the people around you to the nth degree?

When we're faced with losing something or someone special, our appreciation soars. And when you think about it, is there anybody or anything you couldn't lose tomorrow, including your own life?

With that in mind, take a look. What else do you appreciate right now? In this place of profound gratitude, do you see all of creation is special?

Albert Einstein said, "There are only two ways to live in your life. One is as though nothing is a miracle. The other is as though everything is a miracle." Which of these two perspectives serves you the most?

A Universe of Love

Here's another quick adventure into appreciation. Just for a moment, focus on a physical object near to you. We know this object is made of molecules. Molecules are made of atoms

WHAT IF—

*Would you like to have more joy in your life?
Not a fleeting gratification, but waves and waves
of soul-filling joy? Consciously appreciating and
celebrating seems to be the key.*

WHAT IF—

*When we're faced with losing something or
someone special, our appreciation soars. And when
you think about it, is there anybody or anything we
couldn't lose tomorrow, including your own life?*

and atoms are made from protons, neutrons and electrons. We also know that protons, neutrons and electrons are made of even smaller components.

A fundamental question in quantum mechanics, is whether matter is made up of particles or energy. To answer this question, quantum physicists created a fascinating test called the double slit experiment. For our purposes, what makes this experiment extraordinary, is a phenomenon called, "the observer effect," the essence of which is that the process of observing an experiment, in itself, actually impacts the outcome of the experiment. Simply stated, the very presence of an observer, altered the experiment's result.

Now this is a stretch that would most likely have some quantum physicists rolling their eyes, but for our purposes it might be quite useful. Consider the possibility that the most basic essence of these sub-atomic components is neither matter nor energy—but thought itself. And not just thought, but God's thought. And not just God's thought, but God's loving thought.

Consider the possibility that God creates the physical Universe by knowing it into existence and that this knowing comes from a place of unfathomable love.

Now you've got to really open your heart to let this one in. Consider the possibility that the very essence of everything you see, touch, feel, smell or taste is created from God's love. That EVERYTHING you perceive is God telling you, "I love you."

What if the entire physical Universe is an expression of God's love directed specifically to you? Are you willing to let in that much love? And if this is true, how does that affect your level of appreciation for people and the world around you?

WHAT IF—

Everything you see, touch, feel, smell or taste is created from God's love. EVERYTHING you perceive is God telling you, "I love you."

Please pause your reading now for just 30 seconds, look up from this book and notice whatever you see. Let in the experience that whatever you gaze upon is your Creator saying "I love you" in trillions upon trillions of different ways. Consider the possibility that you are quite literally bathed in love every instant of every day and that the opportunity is simply to open your heart to receive it.

I recall visiting a nursing home in Denver on Christmas day. Taking the time to sing some carols and connect with folks who otherwise might not have a single visitor has been such a rewarding tradition for me. On this particular holiday, however, I definitely was the one who received the greater gift.

Walking along the buffed linoleum hallway, I noticed a partially opened doorway and was drawn into the room. As I entered, I saw a frail elderly woman lying on her back, staring at the ceiling through cataract covered eyes.

Before I could say a word, she spoke from the most exquisite soul-centered place, "Isn't life beautiful? Isn't life the most beautiful thing in the world? Oh, it's all just so beautiful!"

I was dumbstruck. Here was this emaciated, old woman too withered to get out of bed. She had everything to complain about, yet here she was resolutely appreciating the gift of life. So intense was her ecstatic state that I chose not to interrupt and left.

Quietly, mesmerized by her presence, I slipped out of her room back into the hallway. Smiling, I re-joined my fellow carolers, humbled and amused at the notion that I was going to cheer HER up!

WHAT IF—

*Whatever you gaze upon is your Creator saying
"I love you" in trillions upon trillions of different ways.
Consider the possibility that you are quite literally
bathed in love every instant of every day and that
the opportunity is simply to open your heart
to receive it.*

An Entire Universe Matrixed Just for You

Here's another perspective that reveals the depth to which we're loved and treasured.

You are unique in all the world. Consider for a moment that out of 7+ billion human beings, you are the ONLY one who sees from behind your eyes. No one else does that.

Now, consider the possibility that nothing in your world has ever happened by accident. Consider the possibility that the entire physical Universe is a perfect multi-dimensional program designed to bring you, moment by moment, exactly the lessons and resources you need to move you up the Wisdom Curve. Every single moment of your life has been perfectly orchestrated to elevate your consciousness. And it's all custom-designed just for you, brought with infinite love.

Now, what if simultaneously, the entire physical Universe is organized to support your best friend in the same extraordinary way? And get this—the Universe that's brought to you and the Universe that's brought to your best friend are matrixed together absolutely flawlessly. From time to time, when both your paths intersect, you have the gift of hanging out with each other for a little while; each of you unconsciously in divine service to the other.

And as if that were not enough, you and your friend's matrixes jive with 7+ billion others. Imagine the brilliance required to create an entire Universe in this way! Wow!

As you open your heart to this cascade of loving, notice your level of prosperity. How prosperous do you feel in this moment? Consider the possibility that real prosperity is not a function of having more. Real prosperity is a function of appreciation. The greater your level of appreciation, the

WHAT IF—

Nothing in your world has ever happened by accident. Consider the possibility that the entire physical Universe is a perfect multi-dimensional program designed to bring you, moment by moment, exactly the lessons and resources you need to move you up the Wisdom Curve.

WHAT IF—

Real prosperity is not a function of having more. Real prosperity is a function of appreciation.

greater your experience of prosperity. So the opportunity is to consciously and deliberately appreciate everything as much as you can as often as you can.

Appreciation Accelerates Heart-Centered Creation

From a spiritual perspective, you don't really have anything you don't appreciate. And anything you do appreciate is yours to experience. As it says in that all-time best seller (specifically in Luke 12:32), "Fear not—for it is your Father's good pleasure to give you the kingdom." Each of us is given the kingdom, not necessarily to own or maintain, but to treasure.

Appreciation also accelerates the upward cycle of heart-centered creation. Because the mind creates in the direction of its focus, the more you appreciate, the more you create the reality that you are cared for. The more you create the reality that you are cared for, the greater your faith. The greater your faith, the more prosperity you generate. The more prosperity you generate, the more you appreciate. For this reason, the most important ingredient in being prosperous (like that little elderly lady) is to notice that you already are.

WHAT IF—

From a spiritual perspective, you don't really have anything you don't appreciate. And anything you do appreciate is yours to experience.

WHAT IF—

Appreciation also accelerates the upward cycle of heart-centered creation. Because the mind creates in the direction of its focus, the more you appreciate, the more you create the reality that you are cared for. The more you create the reality that you are cared for, the greater your faith. The greater your faith, the more prosperity you generate. The more prosperity you generate, the more you appreciate.

Try It Out Exercise: Appreciate

Here are some very simple, fun exercises designed to maximize the power of appreciation. You can do these anywhere and anytime you want to get yourself charged and restored to what's really important. Follow the steps below or you may wish to watch the video titled, "Appreciate:"

www.lcaproject.com/the-opening-videos

First Appreciation Exercise

Step 1:

Create for yourself a quiet time and place where you will be uninterrupted. Light a candle and ask with all your heart to experience the loving presence and assistance of God in this exercise, feeling grateful for knowing your prayer is already answered.

Step 2:

Remember Jimmy Stewart and Donna reed in the film classic "It's a Wonderful Life"? Remember how the angel, Clarence, showed ol' George Bailey how different life would be had he never been born? George got to witness the absence of all the good he had done in his lifetime. In his humility, he begged to go back, to be given another chance. In contrast to his loss, his appreciation for family and friends went through the roof. Great movie!

Imagine for a moment that you lost everything that was precious to you. Make this real in your mind for a moment. What if in an instant you lost everyone in your family, all your money, your home, pets and possessions? What if you lost your freedom, your health, your friends, your career and ability to serve? What if you lost it all and it was going to stay that way? Let this in for a moment. What would that really feel like?

_____

_____

_____

_____

In contrast, how important would the previous day's irritations be, before you lost everything?

_____

_____

_____

_____

_____

Step 3:

Now take a look around you and consciously appreciate what you have. Imagine that everything you see and every person in your world just snapped back—and back as a full expression of God's love for you. What is it like to drink a glass of water? Appreciate it! To hold this book? Appreciate it! To do the dishes? Appreciate it! To pick up after your dog? Appreciate it! To speak to another human being?—

APPRECIATE IT!!!

Step 4:

Take a moment to express gratitude to God for receiving what your soul has been yearning for—a joy-filled relationship with life, steeped in appreciation.

Step 5:

What are you discovering about appreciation?

_____

_____

_____

_____

_____

_____

_____

_____

_____

_____

_____

_____

_____

What is happening in your relationship with God, as you open your heart to appreciate life?

_____

_____

_____

_____

_____

_____

_____

_____

_____

_____

_____

_____

Second Appreciation Exercise

Step 1:

Create for yourself a quiet time and place where you will be uninterrupted. Light a candle and ask with all your heart to experience the loving presence and assistance of God in this exercise, feeling grateful for knowing your prayer is already answered.

Step 2:

Now, let's take it to a deeper level.

Normally, we see ourselves as a physical body navigating its way through the physical Universe, getting stuff done. Let's try on a different perspective.

Imagine being gifted with the most sophisticated video game you've ever experienced. This program is so advanced that you can literally step into it like the Holodeck on Star Trek. It perfectly simulates sight, sound, touch, scent and taste. And it's completely interactive! The shapes and colors are thoroughly realistic. The pitch, depth and volume of sound cannot be distinguished from reality.

As you step into this video game, your surroundings appear to move in extraordinary, 3D replication. When you turn your head, your perspective shifts accordingly and flawlessly. Even your senses of smell and taste are triggered in total alignment with your synthesized environment, and you actually experience the same thoughts and emotions you would feel as if the illusion was real.

Now imagine that this incredible machine is powered by love. By God's love. Imagine that everything you see, hear, touch, smell and taste, is actually being brought to you with tremendous respect and adoration. Like a giant conveyor belt, one experience after another is being delivered, moment by moment with ultimate caring.

Instead of your physically moving in this generated world, this illusion is physically being brought to you, like a bountiful banquet set on a never-ending assembly line. As you hike along a trail, what's really happening is the trail is being presented to you. As you drive your car, the Universe twists and turns beneath your wheels until your destination is delivered.

In other words, imagine everything you perceive, everything you experience, is being brought to you—and IT'S ALL GOOD. It's all God's way of saying, "See, I adore you! See, I'm crazy about you! Always have been and always will! I gave you life so you could enjoy it! So enjoy already!!!"

Step 3:

Now go on a short appreciation walk. Put this book down, go outside and notice the cascade of good brought to you courtesy of God.

Imagine as you walk that you are not the one moving, that the path is being delivered to you beneath your feet. Imagine that everything you see, feel, hear, taste and smell is being brought to you with infinite love.

Savor deeply what you see. Pick something up and feel it. Marvel at its complexity. Listen to the symphony of sounds performed just for you. Drink in fragrances as incense lit in your honor. Taste God's love. Appreciate with all you've got and then come back.

Really do this. Right now! Put the darned book down! Come on! This will be fun! It's only for 5 minutes. You can do this!

On your marks. Get set. Go!!!!!!!!!!!!!!!!!!

Step 4:

Great. Welcome back! What was that like for you?

_____

_____

_____

_____

_____

Step 5:

In this precious space, just take a moment just to say "thank you." Feel the gratitude of receiving insight and direction in experiencing your appreciation.

When you pause to be with God, expressing your gratitude, something wonderful happens. You complete the cycle of giving and receiving. Experiencing and expressing gratitude to a Higher Power reinforces your knowing that you are utterly and completely loved and cared for. In other words, gratitude builds trust.

Would you like to give yourself a treat by pausing now and expressing your thankfulness to God even more? What else are you grateful for, in this very instant?

_____

_____

_____

_____

_____

_____

_____

Celebrate

Celebration isn't just about feeling good—"wooo hoooing" when you're the first one over the finish line. Celebration is downright intelligent. In fact, it's critical for maintaining the machinery of higher consciousness.

Imagine an inner child who lives within you. How do you think this inner child feels about a life devoid of celebration? When your days are just about checking off one item after another and there's no play in between, is it possible something within you might start to rebel? Can you imagine the little kid inside saying, "Forget it! I quit! I'm not playing anymore! Change the program or I'm going to get sick—or create some other kind of drama or emergency!"

When your inner child goes on strike, what happens to your energy level? It's like you just lost half your batteries. Your joy, creativity and aliveness fly out the window and the struggle gets tougher. At best, you're on automatic pilot.

However, when you imbue your life with celebration, your inner child gets with the program. "Oh, we get to play today? We get to celebrate? Cool!!! I'm so on board!!! Come on!!! Let's go!!! Let's go!!!"

Of course, celebrating the biggies is a no brainer. I made that presentation and closed the deal!" Yesssss!!! You're high fiving like you personally won the Super Bowl.

But now imagine the difference in your joy and personal energy if you began celebrating the small stuff—especially the small stuff. You get up in the morning shouting, "Wooo hooo! "I'm alive! I get another day! I tied my shoes! The dishes are put away! My cat's glad to see me! Yaaaa hoooo!

WHAT IF—

*Celebration isn't just about feeling good—
"wooo hoooing" when you're the first
one over the finish line. Celebration
is downright intelligent.
In fact, it's critical for maintaining the
machinery of higher consciousness.*

There's a physiological reason to celebrate as well. When your body is actively moving in celebration, a protein called BDNF (brain-derived neurotropic factor) is having a field day. Dr. James Rouse says, "In as little as 45 seconds of moving your major muscle groups, BDNF improves insulin sensitivity. Your serotonin levels rise and you feel more centered, calm and strong."

The spirit of celebration is also highly contagious. In this arena, my stepmother Stephanie, was a master. She loved to lavish family and friends with music, food and laughter. My father, Bill Ferguson Sr. on the other hand, was the quiet engineer. He was an electronics wizard who could fix just about anything. Put him in a social situation, however, and he was all but lost.

For my Dad's 70th birthday, Stephanie decided to give him a surprise birthday party he would never forget. At the time, they lived in a retirement community in Scottsdale, Arizona.

Brother Bill, Sister Jan and I flew in for the occasion.

When we walked into the oversized clubhouse, we were shocked. The room was packed! I could understand a few folks showing up because Stephanie asked them to—but why in the world would there be so many people there to celebrate Dad's birthday?

The enormous banner that read, "Happy Birthday, Bill!' didn't click in for Dad when he first walked into the room. It wasn't until the crowd stood to their feet yelling "Surprise!!!" that my father began to let in the degree to which he was being honored.

That's when our shock turned into astonishment. Beaming, dad went up to his friends shaking their hands, calling them by name. He danced from table to table laughing, mingling, thoroughly enjoying himself and his guests. Meanwhile, total strangers came up to us and shared what a remarkable and fun-loving man he was.

We stared at Dad. We stared at all his friends. Then we looked at each other bewildered. That's when I asked my brother and sister, "Who is that man and what have they done with our father?"

What none of us realized was that over time, Stephanie's love, encouragement and passion to celebrate, had indeed become contagious. Our wallflower father had broken through the cocoon of his own limiting identity—and blown us all away in the process.

What would happen if you made it a habit to be your own cheerleader, to practice something in the LCA, we call cheer-leadership? We know that the mind creates in the direction of its focus so it's really pretty simple. Just celebrate whatever you want to increase.

What difference will it make as you increase your ability to appreciate and celebrate just 10 percent more in your life? 50 percent more? 100 percent more?

Try It Out Exercise: Celebrate

Dictionary.com defines the word, "joy" as "an emotion of great delight or happiness caused by something exceptionally good or satisfying; keen pleasure; elation." Consider the possibility that joy (or the lack thereof) is, in other words, a function of celebration. It is both a creation and a habit.

Have you ever had your arm in a cast? If so, you know that exercise is required when the cast is removed to overcome the muscle's atrophy. The more you use the muscle, the stronger it gets. As we consciously practice celebration, our ability to feel joy and its frequency, continues to expand.

So if you're serious about experiencing joy more often and more deeply, just follow the steps below or you may wish to watch the video titled, "Celebrate:"

www.lcaproject.com/the-opening-videos

Step 1:

Create for yourself a quiet time and place where you will be uninterrupted. Light a candle and ask with all your heart to experience the loving presence and assistance of God in this exercise, feeling grateful for knowing your prayer is already answered.

Step 2:

Imagine it. Pretend for a moment that you just scratched the last number on your lotto ticket and they all match! You just won the big one!!!!!!!!!!!!!!!!!

Now just for a moment, let your body do what it would do if this was real!

Are you jumping up and down? Are you high fiving and

clapping your hands? What sounds are you making? Are you letting out a huge Wooooohooooo? What is your facial expression? Specifically, notice and write down what your body would do the moment you discovered you really won.

In neuro linguistic programing (NLP), this is called your anchor. The more your mind associates this particular body movement with tremendous joy, the stronger your anchor becomes.

Identifying your anchor can be very useful information. Just as joy stimulates your anchor, your anchor can stimulate the experience of joy. So whenever you especially need that uplifting spirit of celebration, you can demonstrate your anchor to powerfully invoke that feeling! Try it. This really works with practice!

So again, if you won that big lotto, what would your body do in that moment of intense joy? My anchor looks like, sounds like, feels like:

Now, just for the fun of it, for the next few hours—use your anchor to celebrate your accomplishments, big or little. Let your body move and make the sounds just as if you won the lotto—in celebrating the world around you. Who cares if people think you're crazy if it brings you joy?! When you vacuum the rug. Woooo hooooo!!!!! You finish the laundry. Yeeeee haaaaa!!! You clean up your emails. Yessssssss!!!!! Declare it to be Celebration Day in your Universe! Really get into it and watch how the mundane transforms into the miraculous.

Also, the more you celebrate, the more grateful you become. The more grateful you become, the more you feel loved by God. And the more you feel loved by God, the more you know on the deepest level that you are whole and complete regardless of circumstances. Is that cool or what? Yesssssssssssssss!!!!!

Step 3:

Now, if you want, just journal here a bit. What happens to your joy, energy and effectiveness when you use your anchor to celebrate?

_____
_____
_____
_____
_____
_____
_____
_____
_____
_____
_____
_____

How can you apply this tool of celebration in a way that increases both your pleasure and productivity?

_____
_____
_____
_____
_____
_____
_____
_____
_____
_____

What do you notice happens in your relationship with God as you consciously celebrate like crazy?

_____
_____
_____
_____
_____
_____
_____
_____
_____
_____

Step 4:

If you choose, here's an opportunity to give thanks again for your accelerating growth, abundance, wisdom and joy.

THE SACRED SIX:

6 - SERVE

Imagine that you decide to discover the source of a tranquil stream that runs through your mountain village. As you trek deeper and deeper into the forest, you feel the sunlight piercing the old growth canopy, dancing in the tree tops.

For miles you follow the stream's path and are ready to rest when just beneath the spring water's surface, you notice a most unusual rock. As you stare in disbelief, you see a light radiating from the stone that is almost blinding—intense colors that you've never experienced—shooting sparkling rays out into the forest. Mesmerized by its stunning beauty, you kneel to pick it up. That's when it happens.

The instant you grasp the stone, all of your past emotional pain is instantly and permanently released. You feel an indescribable exhilaration as you soar up the Wisdom Curve. The euphoria you experience simply defies comparison and the love you feel for life, yourself and others is without limit. From this level of awareness, you see your greatest potential manifest and the higher destiny of all mankind.

Sprinting now on your journey home, rock in hand with tears of joy running down your cheeks, you meet a friend and share your treasure. His transformation is almost identical to yours! And so it goes with anyone who holds the stone. My question is, from this point forward, to what activity would you dedicate your life?

When our hearts are filled with love for God, ourselves and others—when we surrender and trust—when we listen and follow divine guidance—when we appreciate and celebrate— our spiritual cup becomes filled to overflowing.

Here is where we become naturally compelled to express the last step of the Sacred Six—the opportunity to give back— the opportunity to be part of the flow of infinite providence (provide-ence)—the opportunity to serve.

At this point in our evolution up the Wisdom Curve, when it seems we have reached our capacity to receive more good, when it feels utterly impossible for us to receive more joy, God brings on another wave of it. We ask the question, "How could it get any better than this?" And then, it just does.

Serving others is such a natural expression of our soul. I ask audiences, "For how many of you, does it absolutely make your day when you've had the privilege of making a difference in someone's life?" You can guess their reaction—a sea of upraised hands.

What is your experience when you've shared something that lifts the spirit of another? How does it feel when you've applied that extra effort preparing a meaningful gift for someone? When you actually present it to them, what does that feel like deep inside?

In the famous words of Dr. Albert Schweitzer, "I don't know what your destiny will be, but one thing I know: The only ones among you who will be truly happy are those who have sought and found how to serve."

At this point on the Wisdom Curve, service becomes a way of being. Its foundation is a simple question in which we live. "How can I best contribute in a meaningful way?"

WHAT IF—

*When our hearts are filled with love for God, ourselves
and others—when we surrender and trust—
when we listen and follow divine guidance—
when we appreciate and celebrate—
our spiritual cup becomes filled to overflowing.*

WHAT IF—

*We become naturally compelled to express the last
step of the Sacred Six—the opportunity to give back—
the opportunity to be part of the flow of
infinite providence (provide-ence) —
the opportunity to serve.*

Opening the door for someone. Preparing a meal. Sharing kind words. A touch on the shoulder. Giving financially. Spending time with a new friend. A career of caring. These can all can be sweet acts of service that bring ourselves and others to the front side of the Energy Circle—to the love side of the gate.

God's next invitation for extraordinary good brings forward a possibility for service that we are not usually taught in our culture. It is the possibility that in each of us lives a special expression of serving that resonates with our very soul. It is the invitation to discover our unique life mission.

Discovering Your Life Mission

Your life mission is an ongoing pursuit in service to others that brings you tremendous fulfilment. It's something that pulls you into action, something that taps into talents and potential you already possess. Just the thought of taking this initiative, generates energy within you and puts an enormous smile on your face. It's what you were placed here to do with your life.

However, in our culture, we are not usually offered this possibility. After infancy, you grow up, go to school, get some education, find a job, marry a mate or two, buy a bunch of stuff, retire, grow old and die. Nowhere in this plan are we challenged to discover why we're here.

But if we are graced with the awareness of life mission, the journey to find our unique expression becomes real. As we become engaged in the quest, we learn that manifesting life mission is not so much something created as it is something discovered. In the words of Victor Frankl, "We detect rather than invent our mission in life."

Typically, you won't find your life mission just by looking at the activities of others. Discovering your life mission

WHAT IF—

God's next invitation for extraordinary good brings forward a possibility for service that we are not usually taught in our culture. It is the possibility that in each of us lives a special expression of serving that resonates with our very soul. It is the invitation to discover our unique life mission.

WHAT IF—

"We detect rather than invent our mission in life."
— Victor Frankl

requires that you go within and listen. Like a Geiger counter detects radiation, allow your heart to speak to you when you approach the activities that make your heart sing. Then in your actions, you "try on" the most exhilarating possibilities.

So, armed with an awareness of its possibility, we gain clarity on our mission through the adventure of exploring options. Like trying on garments in a clothing store, we make our best guesses, discovering what fits and what does not. Over time, we learn what activities most resonate with our soul.

I recall a time when my daughter, Heather, asked me for a particular Christmas present. This amazing young lady had successfully initiated efforts to attend the Thatcher School, one of the top equestrian-based prep schools in the nation, and she needed a lead-rope for her mare.

I found a saddlery store in downtown Denver and walked in the front door. That's when it hit me. Standing there in the midst of bridles, saddles, horse blankets, boots and cowboy hats—I was taken aback. The smell of fresh leather brought on a level of joy so intense that it was visceral. I could FEEL it, lifting me up.

Then I remembered as a boy, how I treasured raising Arabian/Quarter horses in southern California. It was a tough time after my parents divorced and these magnificent animal beings brought me through the worst of it.

This joyful remembrance of working with horses has become like a signpost directing me to an essential dream of my heart; owning a ranch in the Colorado foothills. Like Monty, my joy has helped clarify part of my life mission, the importance of being in nature and communing with horses.

Similarly, what is it that lifts you up? What brings you intense joy when you are doing it?

Creating a Life Mission Statement

In our seminars on discovering life mission, I ask participants to create a concise mission statement that contains two ingredients: 1) The activity they most love to do, and, 2) The difference they most want to make in the world.

When I first heard this notion of life mission, I already knew what brought me joy. In addition to my passion for horses, I thrived whenever I had the opportunity to share insights that made a difference, especially in leading personal development seminars. So, I was aware of the activities that I loved, but I didn't know their roles in serving others. I had not yet identified the specific difference I wanted to make.

When I asked my brother how to get started in the seminar business, my mind raced to know, "Where do you get the people? How do you market events? How do you set up the room? What kind of sound system do you need?"

He said, "Randy, stop. You already know what you want to do that brings you joy. Now you need to be clear on the service you want to provide, the difference you want to make." He asked, "What is the communication you want to deliver that will profoundly touch their lives? Find the answer to that question, and all you need to know will follow."

That's when my life mission statement became clear. "To teach personal development seminars that restore people's ability to live in the experience of love—to bring God's children home." Once again, I was furthered by Bill's wisdom.

Here are some examples of mission statements. Notice that each one contains both an activity of joy and an expression of service:

- To compose and perform music in a way that opens people's hearts.

- To teach children history so they become inspired to excel.

- To nurture seniors so they feel valued for their wisdom.

- To provide intelligent counsel so clients experience greater financial freedom.

- To facilitate healing peoples' pain by being with the gentleness of animals.

Over and over again, I've watched folks moved to tears as they crystallize their life mission into a succinct statement. As people get closer and closer to defining their own unique mission, they feel more and more inspired. That's how they know they're on track. It's as if their very soul is proclaiming, "Yes! That's it!! That's what I want to do with my life!!"

I so appreciate L.P. Jacks' quote on work and play:

"The Master in the art of living makes little distinction between his work and his play, his labor and his leisure, his mind and his body, his education and his recreation, his love and his religion. He hardly knows which is which. He simply pursues his vision of excellence in whatever he does, leaving others to decide whether he is working or playing. To him he is always doing both."

Manifesting Your Life Mission

So, what brings you joy and what is the difference you want to make in the world? What is the communication you want to deliver that will impact the people around you? And what difference would it make if you could really do that in your lifetime?

WHAT IF—

A concise purpose statement contains two ingredients:

1. *The activity you most love to do.*
2. *The difference you most want to make in the world.*

WHAT IF—

As people get closer and closer to defining their own
unique mission, they feel more and more inspired.
That's how they know they're on track.
It's as if their very soul is proclaiming, "Yes!
That's it!! That's what I want to do with my life!!"

You don't have to turn your world upside down to begin manifesting your life mission. Barbara Sher says, "There's nothing in the world wrong with keeping a good job and allowing that career to fund what you love." The important thing is to get started.

Jaroldeen Edwards shares this story about beginning the journey.

Several times my daughter had telephoned to say, "Mother, you must come see the daffodils before they are over."

I wanted to go, but it was a two-hour drive from Laguna to Lake Arrowhead. "I will come next Tuesday," I promised, a little reluctantly, on her third call.

Next Tuesday dawned cold and rainy. Still, I had promised, and so I drove there. When I finally walked into Carolyn's house and hugged and greeted my grandchildren, I said, "Forget the daffodils, Carolyn. The road is invisible in the clouds and fog, and there is nothing in the world except you and these children that I want to see bad enough to drive another inch!"

My Daughter smiled calmly and said, "We drive in this all the time, Mother."

"Well, you won't get me back on the road until it clears, and then I'm heading for home!" I assured her. "I was hoping you'd take me over to the garage to pick up my car. How far will we have to drive?"

Just a few blocks," Carolyn said. "I'll drive. I'm used to this."

After several minutes, I had to ask, "Where are we going? This isn't the way to the garage!"

"We're going to my garage the long way," Carolyn smiled, "by way of the daffodils."

"Carolyn," I said sternly, "please turn around."

"It's all right, Mother, I promise—You will never forgive yourself if you miss this experience."

After about twenty minutes, we turned onto a small gravel road and I saw a small church. On the far side of the church, I saw a hand lettered sign that read, "Daffodil Garden."

We got out of the car and each took a child's hand, and I followed Carolyn down the path. Then, we turned a corner of the path, and I looked up and gasped. Before me lay the most glorious sight. It looked as though someone had taken a great vat of gold and poured it down over the mountain peak and slopes. The flowers were planted in majestic, swirling patterns great ribbons and swaths of deep orange, white, lemon yellow, salmon pink, saffron, and butter yellow. Each different colored variety was planted as a group so that it swirled and flowed like its own river with its own unique hue. There were five acres of flowers.

"But who has done this?" I asked Carolyn.

"It's just one woman," Carolyn answered. "She lives on the property. That's her home."

Carolyn pointed to a well kept A-frame house that looked small and modest in the midst of all that glory. We walked up to the house. On the patio, we saw a poster. "Answers to the Questions I Know You Are Asking" was the headline.

The first answer was a simple one. "50,000 bulbs." it read. The second answer was, "One at a time, by one woman, two hands, two feet, and very little brain." The third answer was, "Began in 1958."

There it was, The Daffodil Principle. For me, that moment was a life-changing experience. I thought of this woman whom I had never met, who many decades before, had begun one bulb at a time-to bring her vision of beauty and joy to an obscure mountain top. Still, just planting one bulb at a time, year after year had changed the world. She had created something of ineffable magnificence, beauty, and inspiration.

The principle her daffodil garden taught is one of the greatest principles of celebration. That is, learning to move toward our goals and desires one step at a time— often just one baby step at a time—and learning to love the doing, learning to use the accumulation of time. When we multiply tiny pieces of time with small increments of daily effort, we too will find we can accomplish magnificent things. We can change the world.

"It makes me sad in a way," I admitted to Carolyn. "What might I have accomplished if I had thought of a wonderful goal, thirty-five or forty years ago and had worked away at it 'one bulb at a time' through all those years? Just think what I might have been able to achieve!"

My daughter summed up the message of the day in her usual direct way. "Start tomorrow," she said.

Do It for All of Us

When I was a kid, I'd hear the old folks talking about how quickly life goes by. I'd smile and then leave the room to pursue something far more interesting. At this writing I've reached my senior years and you know what, those old folks were right. It seems like time is accelerating. And if that's true, every day and every moment counts.

Since I've never been as wise as I am right now, this is my chance to give back. This is my chance to share what I've discovered, to give my gift. Regardless of your age, could this be true for you as well?

There is such suffering on the planet. Yet, in sharing this work over three decades, I've seen a trend that gives me great hope. Individuals and organizations are awakening to the possibility of living from a higher place on the Wisdom Curve. They are embracing the notion that what we create on the outside begins with what we create internally. They are realizing that if we are to step into our greatest potential as a species, we need to evolve in our deeper knowing and caring.

Consider the possibility that in doing your own inner work you are actually becoming part of a rising consciousness movement—a family of servers who are doing their part to transform the planet. You shift from a place of "me" to a place of "we." You become like the pioneers of old, but rather than traversing geographical frontier, you are leading the way for others into a frontier of higher awareness. What a glorious adventure!

Sharing your gift of service in the world is, however, not for the timid. There are so many people who have tried and then given up. I believe it was Werner Erhard who said, "For most people, life is what's left over after they've decided they can't make a difference." He also said, "You will move forward in your service when your commitment to make a difference is greater than your fear that you can't."

Maybe what you have to offer is needed more than it's wanted. Offer it anyway. Maybe people will judge you, ridicule you, laugh in your face. See who they are beneath their lack of understanding and love them anyway. Maybe people will be irritated or inconvenienced by your passionate expression of caring. Extend your invitation anyway.

If 10 thousand people turn their heads away and one responds to your service with the courage to be vulnerable and grow, you will know your efforts were entirely worthwhile. Then, when you look back on your life, you can look God in the eye and say, "I took the risks. I served from my heart. Thank you for the opportunity."

This condensed story is from the *New York Times*:

> *During this past year I've had three instances of car trouble: a blowout on a freeway, a bunch of blown fuses and an out-of-gas situation. They all happened while I was driving other people's cars.*
>
> *Each time, when these things happened, I was disgusted with the way people didn't bother to help. I was stuck on the side of the freeway hoping my friend's roadside service would show, just watching tow trucks cruise past me.*
>
> *But you know who came to my rescue all three times? Immigrants. Mexican immigrants. None of them spoke English. One of those guys stopped to help me with*

WHAT IF—

"For most people, life is what's left over after they've decided they can't make a difference."
— Werner Erhard

WHAT IF—

"You will move forward in your service when your commitment to make a difference is greater than your fear that you can't."
— Werner Erhard

the blowout even though he had his whole family of four in tow. I was on the side of the road for close to three hours with my friend's big Jeep. I put signs in the windows, big signs that said, "NEED A JACK," and offered money. Nothing. Just as I was about to give up and start hitching, a van pulled over, and the guy bounded out.

He sized up the situation and called for his daughter, who spoke a little English. He conveyed through her that he had a jack but that it was too small for the Jeep, so we would need to brace it. Then he got a saw from the van and cut a section out of a big log on the side of the road. We rolled it over, put his jack on top and were in business.

I started taking the wheel off, and broke his tire iron. It was one of those collapsible ones. I wasn't careful and I snapped the head clean off. No worries; he ran to the van and handed it to his wife. She was gone in a flash down the road to buy a new tire iron and was back in 15 minutes. We finished the job with a little sweat and cussing (the log started to give), and I was a very happy man.

The two of us were filthy and sweaty. His wife produced a large water jug for us to wash our hands in. I tried to put a twenty in the man's hand, but he wouldn't take it, so instead I went up to the van and gave it to his wife as quietly as I could. I thanked them up one side and down the other. I asked the little girl where they lived, thinking maybe I'd send them a gift for being so awesome. She said they lived in Mexico. They were in Oregon so Mommy and Daddy could pick cherries for the next few weeks. Then they were going to pick peaches, and return home.

After I said my goodbyes and started walking back to the Jeep, the girl called out and asked if I'd had lunch. When I told her no, she ran up and handed me a tamale.

This family, undoubtedly poorer than just about everyone else on that stretch of highway, working on a seasonal basis where time is money, took a couple of hours out of their day to help a strange guy on the side of the road while people in tow trucks were just passing him by.

But we weren't done yet. I thanked them again and walked back to my car and opened the foil wrapped tamale (I was starving by this point). And what did I find inside? My $20 bill.

I whirled around and ran to the van and the guy rolled down his window. He saw the $20 in my hand and just started shaking his head no. All I could think to say was, "Por favor, por favor," with my hands out. The guy just smiled and, with what looked like great concentration, said in English: "Today you, tomorrow me."

Then he rolled up his window and drove away, with his daughter waving to me from the back. I sat in my car eating the best tamale I've ever had, and I just started to cry. It had been a rough year; nothing seemed to break my way. This level of kindness was so out of left field I just couldn't handle it.

In the several months since then I've changed a couple

of tires, given a few rides to gas stations and once drove 50 miles out of my way to get a girl to the airport. I won't accept money. But every time I'm able to help, I just remember, "Today you, tomorrow me."

How might the world be different if we simply loved one another? What would change if we lived in the spirit of service, in the spirit of "Today you, tomorrow me?"

WHAT IF—

The world might be different if we simply loved one another. What would change if we lived in the spirit of service, in the spirit of "Today you, tomorrow me?"

Try It Out Exercise:
Discovering Life Mission,
Your Unique Expression of Service

You might want to watch the video titled: The Miracle of Service. Doing so, will expand your knowledge of life mission and clarify your own mission statement. Discovering this aspect of yourself is such a vital key to long-term fulfilment.

www.lcaproject.com/the-opening-videos

Here's the exercise:

Step 1:

There is great wisdom in first asking how you can serve God, before asking God to serve you. Here is a simple prayer for direction.

> *God, You are the creator of all that is. You are the epitome of love, peace, power, presence, prosperity and wisdom. You are my Source, my beginning and end, and You live right in the center of my heart. Thank You so much for that.*

> *God, I give You my life. I surrender all that I have and all that I am to You. And in this place of surrender, I trust that You will continue to care for me completely.*

> *God, I am listening with all my heart. Please reveal my life mission to me. What do You want me to do with this life You have provided? How do You want me to serve?*

> *God, from the bottom of my heart, I thank You for this priceless gift of becoming clear on my divine direction.*

> *Thank You! Thank You! Thank You! And so it is.*

Step 2:

Please list the activities in your life that bring you the most joy. Notice how just creating this list lifts your heart.

_____

_____

_____

_____

_____

_____

_____

_____

Step 3:

If you could deliver a specific communication or make a positive difference on the planet, what would that look like? What would that service be?

_____

_____

_____

_____

_____

_____

Step 4:

Now is your chance to get creative! Using your answers above, complete your mission statement with those two main ingredients: what you most love to do, and how you can serve others by doing it. (Suggestion: Be succinct. The fewer the words, the easier it is to internalize). As I shared, you'll know you're on track when just reading your mission statement, touches your heart.

My mission statement is:

_____

_____

_____

_____

_____

_____

Step 5:

In this sacred space—once again feel that magnificent Light glowing within you and filling your whole body with immeasurable loving—and ask for counsel. Be still and listen. What is His advice on the next action steps required to express your mission in the world?

_____

_____

_____

_____

_____

_____

_____

_____

_____

_____

_____

_____

_____

Step 6:

Are you willing to follow His guidance?

What action steps are you committed to taking so more and more, you are expressing your life mission in the world? And how will you manage this transition in a way that works?

Step 7:

Take a moment to express gratitude for clarifying your mission statement, the most fulfilling expression of soulful service.

HOW TO CREATE
YOUR OWN GOD JOURNAL

The notion of actually being in communication with God, can bring up some interesting reactions in people. What would folks think if you told them you are in direct, two-way communication with the Almighty?

"Oh yea, you talk to God. Sure you do."

"Personally, I think you're losing it."

"Wait right here while I go get some nice folks who can help you."

Such are the thoughts from a culture steeped in spiritual skepticism, a culture that defines sanity as successful compliance with the norm.

Yet, when you are in the experience of your loving, being in communication with God is completely right and natural. If our Heavenly Father adores His children, of course He is going to be in communication with you!

I recall the parable Christ shared of the prodigal son. "But while he was still a long way off, his father saw him and was filled with compassion for him; he ran to his son, threw his arms around him and kissed him." (Luke 15:20). The father didn't say, "Oh look, the slacker has come crawling back." No! Instead he was moved with gratitude and compassion. And he RAN to him!

When you look deep in your heart, how does it feel to be loved to this degree and beyond? Again, I have no proof we are treasured this profoundly or that God wants to be in communication with us, but it's a reality that could be quite useful, isn't it?

What Happens When You Commune With God?

Consider the possibility that God is your ultimate resource. If you break down the word resource, it becomes Re-Source—to reconnect with Source, that special something we've been searching for forever, that sweet nectar that quenches our spiritual thirst like nothing else can. So imagine the enormity of communicating directly with God on a daily basis. What would be the benefits to you?

- You would be living in genuine partnership with an all-knowing, all-powerful, all-present, all-loving, all-available Creator. It seems to me it would be difficult to find a better Re-Source.

- You would experience a profound sense of peace, knowing on the deepest level that God is perpetually there for you and that you can always count on His loving presence.

- You would receive divine guidance in your daily actions. How would that affect your life direction and productivity?

- You would have a deep sense of living on track—knowing you are right where you need to be, taking the very best actions, all in right timing.

- Bitterness and separation spawned from harshly judging self and others, would be replaced by an experience of compassion and oneness.

- Comparing yourself negatively to others would fall away as would your addiction to appearing successful. These two time-wasters would become ridiculously irrelevant.

- You wouldn't have to figure everything out by yourself. You wouldn't have to fight to control, elbowing your way to success with impossible-to-maintain standards. What a relief!

- Because of your spiritual orientation, you would soar up the Wisdom Curve becoming truly effective. No longer would you have to stay stuck in old patterns, taking years to learn your lessons.

- You would be joyful most of the time. You would get back your hope. You would be living in the Light.

- You would shift from believing in God to experiencing God, carrying Him in your heart in all that you do.

These are just a few of my ideas. What other benefits do you see in being in direct two-way communication with God?

_____
_____
_____
_____
_____
_____
_____
_____
_____
_____
_____
_____
_____
_____
_____

It's a big step from doubting or denying the existence of God, to actually believing in Him. Perhaps it's just as big a step from believing in God, to living with Him in your heart. If your deepest desire is to experience oneness with God and feeling His presence in all you do, there is a way to bring this forward. I know of no better method to create this level of spiritual intimacy than to be in frequent heart to heart communication with God. Keeping a God Journal is a wonderful means of accomplishing this and it's really pretty simple.

Here's How I Do It

I do not know if what works for me is going to work for you, so please adapt the following steps according to your own sense of integrity and what resonates in your own heart.

Here's how I do it.

1. Early, most every morning, before my mind clutters with the day's have-to-do list, I go into the privacy of my sacred place, light a candle and kneel next to a little altar above which is a beautiful framed drawing of Jesus.

2. I create the experience of the Sacred Six; a place of love, surrender, trust, heart-centered listening, willingness to follow His guidance, appreciation, celebration, and desire to serve. Creating this state of consciousness, opens the door to the temple of profound communication.

3. Then I enter into prayer. I simply ask God to help me open my heart so I can be with Him. By the way, however you express yourself in prayer is just fine. It's just being in conversation.

WHAT IF—

It's a big step from doubting or denying the existence of God, to actually believing in Him. Perhaps it's just as big a step from believing in God, to living with Him in your heart.

I know some people who pray like poets. Their words flow like music. But that's not what really matters when it's just you and God in your sacred time. Just talk with Him. There's no one judging.

4. After that, I read a little scripture and something else that inspires me.

5. I turn to a fresh new page in my God Journal and write the date. Then I simply write, "Good Morning, God."

6. In this sacred moment, I pause and listen with all my heart. Usually, God responds with "Good Morning, Randy." And I write that down.

7. At this point, if He doesn't have anything to immediately say to me, I share succinctly what I'm going through (well aware He already knows) and ask direct questions about anything.

8. In this loving space, He replies with the most exquisite wisdom and I record His words on the page.

9. Back and forth we dialogue until We feel a sense of completion.

10. When We've finished, I usually say thank you or share how much I love Him. Often, he does the same.

Then I launch my day, doing my best to apply His counsel.

How do I know that I'm truly in conversation with God? I don't. But as you know, I am no longer bound by what is provable.

WHAT IF—

You just talk with Him.
There's no one judging.

But what if God tells me to do something horrible?—like the crazies in the news who explain to police, "God told me to do it."

He won't do that. If you hear guidance along that line, don't do it because it's not God speaking. His very nature is love itself. Yes, He's asked me to make difficult decisions, but He's never asked me to step into judgment or be deliberately hurtful.

How Do I Know It's God Speaking?

Over the years I've seen some very specific patterns to God's guidance. Here are 12 consistent qualities that tell me it is He who is sharing:

1. His words always come from a place of great love—straight forward but never harsh, condescending or punitive. I once asked him about this in my God Journal. His response blew my socks off. It was so direct, so powerful, and touched me to the core. He said, "I do not punish! Why would I resist My own creation?"

2. He speaks from a place of certainty, consistency and wisdom far beyond my own.

3. He speaks my language both literally and philosophically. He knows where I am in my consciousness and connects with me in that place.

4. Sometimes His counsel is very general like, "Stay close to Me and live the Sacred Six today." Sometimes He's very specific like, "Clean up the garage. Follow up on that conversation. Apologize to your friend. Begin the outline for Our new book."

WHAT IF—

What if God tells me to do something horrible?

He won't do that.
If you hear guidance along that line, don't do it
because it's not God speaking.

5. His guidance always feels like the right thing to do, although it often takes me beyond my comfort zone.

6. Without exception, the result of doing as He asks, ultimately turns out to be the very best for all concerned (although not everyone may initially feel that way).

7. Following his counsel doesn't always give me what I want, but ultimately it always, always gives me what I need to evolve.

8. In following His guidance, I grow tremendously. He takes me to places up the Wisdom Curve I would never attain on my own.

9. With His guidance, I can see a bigger picture, becoming more skilled as an effective instrument of service.

10. The more I ask for His counsel, the more He speaks. The more He speaks, the more I hear. The more I hear, the more I know. The more I know, the better action I take. The better action I take, the more fulfilled I become.

11. When we're finished, I always feel restored; reconnected to what is good, pure, important and real.

12. In my obedience, God and I grow closer and closer over time.

When I don't know what to do, I ask one of two questions. The first is, "What is the greatest expression of love for myself and others?"

The second question is "God, what do you want me to do?"

Interestingly enough, I find that the answers to both of these questions are consistently identical.

Straight from Randy's God Journal

Here are some examples from my journal. Just be prepared; my humanness can be as scratchy as my penmanship:

6 / 1 / 06

Good Morning God,

It's the first day of June and the sun has not yet peeked over the horizon. What beautiful silence your morning brings. Lord, my heart is full of peace, and a rich sense of joyful anticipation. Thank you for loving me. How can I serve? How can I give today?

Dear dear Randy, your greatest gift to me is simply being. That you would know me and love me is icing on the cake. Oh, how I love my children... _all_ of my children. Every_one_ and every thing matters to me. In fact matter exists only because it matters to me... matter exists only because of my loving.

Randy, you are on the right path... a _most_ exquisite path.

Continue to grow in your loving,
in your passion to give. I'll handle the
money. Stay with me here, Randy.
Live the life you teach. Teach the
life you live. Anticipate my good
for you. I love you more than you
know

Oh Father, my precious Lord. Thank
you for this gift of life. Thank you for
being a loving God. Thank you for loving
me!!!

In this entry, God and I are simply treasuring each other's presence. Like two lovers lost in ecstatic dance, celebrating eternity in a single breath.

I especially enjoy hearing how all of creation matters to Him and exists by virtue of His loving. Then He challenges me to a new level of authenticity. In his words: "Live the life you teach and teach the life you live."

Wednesday February 1, 2012

Oh Father, good Morning

Good Morning, Randy.

Lord, Janny said yesterday that Mom just has a few days left with us.

Oh Father, I have such a sadness in my heart.

Randy, I understand completely. It's OK. One day, you will join me in Heaven and experience joy, bliss, freedom and peace beyond anything you can now imagine. And when that happens, you will feel such joy when those who follow you make their transition.

It is a good thing ... a very good thing.
Virginia is in my arms. She

has had a place in my heart always. Just like you.

Truly, Randy, it is all good. Very, very good.

Mom passed on the 12th of February that year. Hearing these words helped me navigate through my grieving in the most beautiful way. In His sharing, any notion of death as something awful, gives way to simply appreciating the time I got to spend with her.

Friday January 18, 2013

Good Morning, Lord.

Good Morning, Randy.

Oh Father, yesterday You asked me to work on the divorce and I didn't do it. I deliberately didn't do it... and my procrastination felt awful. I'm sorry, Lord.

Randy, when I ask you to do something, you always have the option to disregard my counsel. This is part of the free will I have given you.

But if I step away from Your path, there are consequences.

Yes. There are always consequences, regardless of your choice.

I step out of the Light?

My precious son, you are _always_ in My Light. You just close your eyes to it... and things happen when you travel with your eyes shut.

It's OK, son. All my children close their hearts to My loving... with rare exceptions. I do not judge you. I invite you... and you get to choose. That is all.

Oh Father, thank you for a new day. Please help me to live in Your Light, the Light of Your Holy Spirit.

Yes, Randy. I will.

Lord, how would You counsel me today?

Randy, pray with all your heart to feel close to Me... to live the Sacred Six... and all will be added unto you.

Yes, Father.

Love your clients. Forgive and love Gail. Release what you had with her, to Me. Give Me your tears as you let her go.

Yes, Lord.

Then feel My peace and your joy will return. This is My counsel for you today.

Yes, Father. I will follow your counsel. Thank you for loving me so.

That, my son, you can always count upon.

:) :)

There is such an absence of judgment and manipulation in His counsel. And boy, does He get to the point fast. "My precious son, you are always in My Light. You just close your eyes to it—and things happen when you travel with your eyes shut."

There's also such relief in knowing that I'm not alone in my blundering. Over and over again, we all make mistakes. And yet, we're welcomed back instantly.

"I do not judge you. I invite you. And you get to choose. That is all."

Wednesday October 23, 2013

Good Morning, Lord.

Good Morning, Randy.

Oh Father, this morning I feel something like loneliness... a yearning to be deeply loved... touched... honored... loved... desired... wanted. It is as if there is an emptiness inside, these feelings can fill.

Lord, I have felt this yearning so much of my life and tried to fill it with the presence of women... real and imagined.

Oh Lord, how would You counsel me about this?

Precious Randy, all of My children have this yearning to be loved... some feel it more acutely than others. Few are aware of its true dynamics.

My son, what you are feeling is a profound yearning to be one with Me. It is divine... part of My Holy design.

You yearn for the Way, the Truth,

the Light. You yearn for fulfillment that only I can provide.

To fulfill this yearning, open your heart to receive My love.

Yes, this yearning abates in being with another person. But they are NOT the Source of your fulfillment any more than a wire is the source of electricity. And when you forget this truth, you invite a lesson that can be painful. The person leaves and you feel as if you've lost love itself.

You haven't, though. You've just had your heart pryed open to know the truth.

Randy, I am what your heart yearns for. All the love you've ever needed or wanted is right before you, forever and ever without fail.

So when you ache for the loving touch of a woman... know it is Me who your soul most desires.

Love Me Randy. Be with Me.

Adore Me and you will receive the most perfect love, being and adoration.

I promise you, miracles will come if you follow My counsel.

Yes, Lord. Please help me stay anchored in this awareness. Please give me all that is needed to follow Your will.

I have. I am. And I will.

Thank You, Lord.

How may I serve You today?

Look in your heart and mind. Choose your best path. I am with you.

I love You, Father.

⌣ ⌣

In my painful moments, He is there for me. Always. In this case, God offers a beautiful reframing of loneliness as a yearning for meaningful spiritual connection. He makes it clear that He is source, not a relationship with anyone or anything external. So what I yearn for, I already have.

Thursday October 16, 2014

Good Morning, Lord

Good Morning, Randy.

Oh Father, I did as You asked yesterday. I set aside my dilemas and just loved You intensely. I loved You as I counseled Our clients. I loved You in the afternoon and evening. And it was good Lord... very good.

Father, You brought us a new paying client. Thank You.

Lord, I feel like I'm experiencing at least a little glimmer of what You have been telling me for so long. You really are the Way, the Truth and the Life and Light of the world... the Living God

Yes, Randy, I really am.

And I don't have to prove myself to anyone?

That's right, My son. You are accountable only to Me, your Creator... not to earn My love and respect, for these you already have beyond measure.

You are accountable to Me to evolve, to grow up the wisdom curve, to become Christ-like in your human journey. You are accountable to fulfill your destiny in divine partnership with Me

You are accountable to grow organically, to open your heart and ride the wave of life I continually provide.

Randy, I love you so. I yearn to give to you. Open yourself to My treasure. Do this through your loving.

Oh God, thank You. I'm starting to get it. So many insights are flowing now.

It's not about filling the LCA. It's about sharing a magnificent gift.

Oh God, I love You so much. And today I will love You more.

That, Randy, is a great business plan.

‿ ‿

Here, God clarifies His expectations for me. It isn't about making it big in man's eyes. And it sure isn't about being "sinless." It's about going for it. Listening to Him and doing my best. It's about evolving as a being through my participation in the direction of perfection. Thank you God, for ground rules I can work with.

Monday June 13, 2016

Good Morning, Lord

Good Morning, Randy.

Oh Father, I place such importance on the circumstances, like getting lost in a movie as opposed to being delightfully separate... and entertained by it.

Oh Father, help Me to be in the world but not of the world.

Randy, this is a vastly intelligent request.

Come to Me, My son. Feel Me in Your heart this day. Live the sacred six and be nurtured in Our love.

Yes, fill Your cup with the nectar of the Truth. Only in this way will You ever find what Your soul seeks.

I feel it now, Lord.

Good. Welcome back.

Randy, obedience to Me is a gift to You. It is the how-to... moment by moment... to live the richness of My kingdom.

Live this different way of being today and You will know how to complete Our book.

Yes, choose which shall be Your master; Me... or My creation. One is life. One is death.

Yes, Lord. I choose You. You are the way... the truth... the Light and life.

Yes, I am.

I so respect how God always honors my free will to choose between seeing Him as primary cause, or the circumstances. He always gives me the right to choose. Also, the way He positions obedience as a gift "to live the richness" is especially useful.

Friday August 19, 2016

Good Morning, Lord.

Good Morning, Randy.

Lord, yesterday I consciously broke My promise with You to escape and feel good for a little while.

Oh God, the separation is excruciating. It's not worth it.

Do You really see that, Randy?

Yes, Lord. It hurts. It throws Me Back. Then I have to dig My way back to recover. It's an enormous waste of time, life and energy.

It's also contributed to the end of 3 marriages

Yes, Randy. It is as You say

Oh My Lord, how would You counsel Me?

Are You really asking for help?

I am, Lord.

Okay. Then just stop it. Redirect your focus.

I promise, Father. I give You My word.

Know that to break this promise is a hard fall. To keep it is to progress.

Yea, Lord.

Good. Lets move on.

Today, be with Me in your appointments. Hold Me closely, Randy.

Yea, Lord.

This weekend, make your calls. Speaking calls today. CTL and CTLA calls today and tomorrow.

See what needs to be done and do it. That will feel much better.

Dig in. Stoke. Connect. Determine.

I will, Lord.

Often, God gives me very direct coaching on action to take. He tells it like it is and in this case, directs me to "Just stop it" when it comes to self-inflicted suffering. Then He offers counsel on specific priorities.

Without exception, I notice that following his advice on top priorities makes for a better day in a big way.

Tuesday November 22, 2016

Good Morning, Lord

Good Morning, Randy.

Oh Father, this morning I woke up a bit on the back side of the Energy Circle. Then, immediately I shifted to the front side & began asking forward focused questions involving my body, mind and emotions.

Lord, I literally created being in a great mood. Thank You for that miracle! Thank You for the knowing that I don't ever have to go to that dark place unconsciously again... or stay there

Lord that is a miracle! Thank You, Lord.

Randy, You are welcome. Yes, let in that Joy. This is a powerful place of consciousness We have attained, in You, together.

Oh God! The miracles that lay ahead!

Yes, Randy. This changes everything doesn't it?

Yes, Lord. Oh Father, how may I serve You today?

Stay in this place of deep, joyful connection.

Radiate My Light... Your Light... Our Light.

Embrace Your joyfulness and let the good times roll! For all My times are good indeed.

Oh Father, I accept Your invitation.... Your
enormous gift of love for me. Thank You!

:)

Today, Randy, love My children. Let them
know that I love them with the full power
of the God of the Universe. For all time.

I will, Lord I'll do that today.

Good. I am with You. In You. As You.

Enjoy!

:) :)

This conscious shift in attitude was a major victory for me. In the past, if I awoke in a bad mood, my entire day would be compromised. But this time, that didn't get to happen. I took dominion over a backward focus and anchored the knowing that I can do this at any time for the rest of my days.

If I have the power to shift my thought in this way, how much more can I live the Sacred Six? How closely can I align my life with God's will in the moment? And what are the miracles that will come from this transformation?

Thursday June 1, 2017

Good Morning, Lord.

Good Morning, Randy.

Oh Father, I am back... ready to work... to play...
to do Your will.

Randy, keep the richness... the peace of Your time
in Costa Rica. Prioritize with Me and take right
action as a moving meditation. Yes, live in Your
deep gratitude to Me and enjoy this day.

Yes, Lord. I will.

Father?

Yes.

Jesus had no possessions. He loved, gave, healed,
challenged, was crucified and arose. He said to
go out and preach the Gospel. He invited people to
give up their possessions and follow Him.

My Lord, do You want Me to sell everything...
pay off My debt... to give what I have to the poor
...to be as Your disciples... as Christ?

No, Randy. That is not Your path. I want You to
build Our LCA. I want You to walk Your talk.

Jesus didn't ask people to give away all that they
had. He asked people to surrender first... to love
the Lord their God. He asked them to live the
Sacred Six. He asked people to see from the eyes
of love.

Randy, His path is not Your path. You are not the Christ. You are Tonopah... man through whom My Spirit lives.

Live the Sacred Six and all is revealed. Live the Sacred Six and receive the instruction I have for You. This is My desire for You, My son.

Thank You, Lord. Oh Father, thank You!

:)

Lord, how may I serve You this beautiful kt day of June.

Be clear on Our steps for expansion. Hire Our CRD. Get Our book out there to My Children. Hire Our consultants.

Go for it Randy with gusto, grace, prosperity and ease.

Give it Your all... Your very best!

Enjoy.

Yes, Father

Oh God, I'm so grateful.

:) :)

The lessons I learned on my trip to Costa Rica were about self-care; specifically, the importance of periodically getting away and restoring. He's asking me to do this regularly.

God is also clarifying my path. He doesn't want me to lead a life of material austerity but rather a life of abundance, all in right perspective—as he says, "through the eyes of love." He also is asking me to hire more staff, to give the LCA everything I've got, and to enjoy the journey.

What is Your Next Step?

So, your mission, should you decide to accept it, is to get a fresh new journal and just begin. Give it a shot. And know that your experience will be unique to you. If nothing happens right away, don't give up. Keep knocking at the door, asking with all your heart, and it will be opened for you.

I once read a story on a tea box. Perhaps you have seen Warner Sallman's painting of Christ in a garden, knocking on a wooden door.

There is a story about the artist when he first unveiled his work. Some of the critics who were present began to laugh. Perplexed at their reaction, the artist asked why they were laughing.

At that point, the spokesman replied, "We're laughing because you forgot to paint a handle on the door so it could be opened.

That was when the artist replied, "My dear friends, this is the door to the human heart and it can only be opened from the inside."

WHAT IF—

My dear friends, this is the door to the human heart and it can only be opened from the inside.

STEPPING INTO MASTERY

I recall the day I was asked to teach a special little girl how to ride her bike without training wheels. This little one was scared but determined. After some encouragement, she wobbled off about 30 yards and ran into a curb. She took her spill, moved through the tears then climbed right back on her bike.

She had grown to a point where training wheels were no longer acceptable and knew there was a higher possibility. The pull to master the next level, to ride with her friends on just two wheels, was relentless for her. Her old way of riding was simply no longer tolerable.

In the same way, God's invitation for us to evolve in consciousness is both inevitable and continual. When we blow it in life, when we run into curbs as we all do, the opening to expand is there for us over and over again.

What's Your Life Worth?

Here's a crazy question for you. How much is your life worth?

Imagine for a moment, a finely dressed gentleman came to you, checkbook in hand and said, "Here's the deal. I'm going to write you a check for any amount of money you request, and my bank will indeed pay you that sum. Really."

You gasp. Then you smile, contemplating an amount because you know he is quite serious.

The gentleman pauses, adjusts his tie and continues, "All I ask in return is that whatever number of days you have left to live on the planet be instantly transferred from your life account into mine. Now, what amount should I write on the check?"

Most likely at this point, your answer is an emphatic, "No deal!" You may even have the inclination to tell this dude precisely where he can put his checkbook.

As silly as this example may at first appear, it has meaning. It establishes value. In other words, isn't the time you have left to live between right now and when you take your last breath, absolutely priceless? And if that's true, how do you want to spend this infinitely precious asset?

In the limited time you have left on earth, how much aliveness do you really want out of your life? How strong is your yearning to experience love deeply in your heart? How vital is it to you, to discover and deliver the gifts you were meant to share with the world? How important is it to you to feel close to God?

After years of being on this path, I've come to a conclusion. I am both pathetically and magnificently human. I've learned that peace doesn't come in finally being good enough, smart enough, successful or loved enough. We will never, ever, ever, accumulate enough evidence on the outside to prove we're not who we've judged ourselves to be on the inside.

Determining Your Priority

My brother speaks about the importance of priorities and he shares it well. He says there are two distinct and opposite directions to go in life.

One way is to crown the circumstances of your life as king, making them your *number one* priority. This is devoting your life primarily to doing and accumulating—arranging

WHAT IF—

*Peace doesn't come in finally being good enough,
smart enough, successful or loved enough.
We will never, ever, ever, accumulate enough
evidence on the outside to prove we're not who
we've judged ourselves to be on the inside.*

your career, finances, property, cars, education, reputation, spouse, kids, and other things in just the right way.

There are some big problems with this orientation. When we make arranging the circumstances king, we have to gear down our relationship with God. This is true because the mind can only focus on one thing at a time. You can't serve two masters.

In choosing this first option, we set aside our peace, love, joy and trusting in order to accomplish. We live in the question, "What must I do next?" And that is what life becomes fundamentally about; doing. Do, do, do!

Also, in this modality, we're never able to get enough of what we don't have. The list always grows faster than our ability to check the items off. No matter how much we achieve or accumulate, it needs to be more, faster, better or different. So in the end, we compromise our connection with God, AND we're never fully satisfied with our circumstances.

In the second and opposite option, Spirituality is our number one priority. When we make this direction our primary orientation, great things happen. We receive all the gifts of being in relationship with God instantly. We live in the flow of life in a state of profound peace, love, joy and trusting most of the time. Ironically, our effectiveness actually increases. Our "doing" comes first from "being," so we become more effective as leaders, parents, teachers and friends. As Steven Covey shares, "Not only do we have the right ladder, but we know it's leaning against the right wall." We live in a profound state of appreciation and contentment for what we already have. With this alternate focus, we get God AND we're incredibly satisfied with our circumstances.

Bottom line: We have the choice of losing closeness to God and losing deep satisfaction with life, or having closeness to God and having deep satisfaction with life. It's one or the other. The Opening is an invitation to choose wisely.

So, which is it for you? I love this quote by Thoreau, "If you have built castles in the air, your work need not be lost; that is where they should be. Now put the foundations under them."

Slowly I am learning that "being" trumps "doing" all day long. So rather than devoting my primary focus to getting stuff done so someday I'll feel love, I'm learning to love, so I have the wisdom to get the right stuff done.

Sometimes in my journaling, God share's incredibly powerful one-liners that throw me back in my chair.

I recall one very busy morning taking a few minutes to connect with Him. I wrote, "God, I so treasure feeling close to you. But in just a few minutes I'm going to be immersed in a packed agenda. There's so much I have to get done today and I'm concerned about losing You in all my activity. Lord, how would you counsel me?"

To which He zinged me with this one. God said simply, "Randy, First love—Then do."

Wow! So simple. So clear.

The Courage to Hope Big

Over years of practicing the Sacred Six, I have discovered something quite astounding. I've learned without exception, that when people drop their fear, guilt, resentment, attachment and judgment (all their primary sources of pain and separation), what they discover is that who they are, is love itself. They experience a deep, organic adoration for themselves and every human being on the planet.

This phenomenon doesn't seem so much to be a new creation as it is a discovery of a pre-existing truth. Consider the possibility that as a species, we already love one another intensely. It's living incongruently with this truth that generates our suffering. That's why we feel such heaviness when the news brings us the latest atrocity. It's also what bonds us in the wake of natural disasters. The hurting of a few affects us all because truly we are one, living in singular bodies. As Teilhard de Chardin said, "We are not human beings having a spiritual experience. We are spiritual beings having a human experience."

This brings up an extraordinary possibility. As we continue to evolve up the Wisdom Curve individually and collectively, we mature towards a world culture where every person matters.

When I ask people to imagine a world where our fundamental motivator is a genuine caring for one another, their most common first reaction is, "That's great, Randy, but it's sure not going to happen in my lifetime." I imagine that is because, as a culture, we've been hurt so many times that to hope for world peace feels like counting on winning the lotto. We are afraid to be disappointed again, so we're reluctant to hope.

But what if we're already evolving in that direction? Most people never questioned that the earth was flat until the third century

WHAT IF—

Bottom line: We have the choice of losing closeness to God and losing deep satisfaction with life, or having closeness to God and having deep satisfaction with life.
It's one or the other.
The Opening is an invitation to choose wisely.

WHAT IF—

"First love—Then do."
—God

B.C. when Hellenistic astronomy confirmed what we know today. What if, as we look back from the future, we see that man developed from the Stone Age, to the Agricultural Age, to the Industrial Age, to the Information Age, to the Age of Awareness?

Consider the possibility that as more and more people embrace living the Sacred Six, two beautiful outcomes occur. First, whoever lives this way gets what this way gives. Second, whoever lives this way, becomes a radiant example of possibility in the world. What if this enlightened way of being grows person by person into a critical mass that in turn, liberates even more of the people around us?

WHAT IF—

Whoever lives this way becomes a radiant example of possibility in the world. What if this enlightened way of being grows person by person into a critical mass that in turn, liberates even more of the people around us?

Living the Sacred Six

What might be the power in having the Sacred Six as a foundation for the castles you have already created? Are you willing to take on the challenge of living the Sacred Six?:

1. Are you willing to *love God* with all your heart, soul, mind and strength?

2. Are you willing to *love yourself and others* with all your heart, soul, mind and strength?

3. Are you willing to *surrender* your attachments, your will, your very life and are you willing to *trust* that people and circumstances are the way they are, knowing that you are absolutely cared for?

4. Are you willing to *listen* deeply and *follow* His guidance?

5. Are you willing to *appreciate and celebrate?*

6. And are you willing to *serve*, to have your life be about giving?

In our process of spiritual evolution, we will forget. We will remember. Then forget and remember again. In this process, we evolve. All the while, love is there to catch us, teach us, heal us and eventually to bring us home to who we truly are.

Thank you for sharing this special time with me. I love you with all my heart, soul, mind and strength.

— Randy

IN APPRECIATION

I recall my father once saying, "I am absolutely amazed how well you three kids turned out, given the way I parented." His humility was both healing and revealing. It felt good to hear him take ownership for mistakes he'd made in raising us. His comment also revealed his commitment to straightforward communication. I could always count on him to tell it like it was.

As an engineer, dad taught me how things work. He taught me order, systems and logic. He taught me values and how to navigate in the physical world. Thanks, Dad.

Mom taught me about love and service. She modeled the very best of Christianity and had an amazing ability to appreciate. When I was in her presence I always felt treasured, enjoyed and seen for the person I truly am. What an amazing gift! Her vibrant love for life inspired new friendships wherever she went.

When I was a newborn, I had something called pyloric stenosis, a severe stomach ailment that took me to the edge of death. At one point Mom said, "God, if you let Randy live, I will give my life to you in service." I survived and Mom devoted over 50 years of her life serving the church and surrounding community.

To this day it's hard for me to get my arms around how much her love for us fueled her patience. One day I stole $10 out of her purse. This was when, as a single mom, she was raising three kids and paying a mortgage on $375/month. A few days later, I told her my good fortune of finding $10 on the ground. She looked right at me, paused, and replied, "That's nice, Honey."

That was all she said. When she wasn't looking, I put the money back in her purse. Thanks Mom for showing me the power in love-based wisdom.

We call my younger sister Saint Jan. She clearly inherited Mom's DNA for authentic caring. Janny's reputation for dispensing wisdom and her capacity for heart-centered listening is legendary. I think when we all get to heaven, I'll have to travel quite a distance to get to her neighborhood (I hope they let me in). Thanks, Jan, for your passionate ongoing advocacy.

Then there's brother Bill, my extraordinary mentor. This is the same guy who wrote the forward to this book. Bill has a remarkable ability to see how we operate as human beings. He's also masterful in communicating the possibility of life in a way that transforms people's lives. My guess is that God is still paying dividends from when Mom gave her life to Him. Why else would I be so blessed with a brother I adore who does the same kind of work I do? Bill, more than any human being on the planet, you have molded my consciousness into what it is today. Check him out for yourself at:

www.MasteryofLife.com

Thanks to my daughter, Heather, for your cut-to-the-chase worldly wisdom. I am continually blown away in the joy you receive in parenting my two scrumptious grandchildren. What a remarkable old soul you are. I recall a time when you were little. Your Mom and stepdad, were having an argument. In the heat of the moment, your Mom asked which side you were on. Your reply was profound. You looked her straight in the eye and said, "Well, I'm not on your side. And I'm not on his side. I'm on the side of Spirit." I think that ended the argument.

There are so many other people to thank. Steven Vannoy has been such a stellar example of heart-centered leadership. Our long-standing friendship is one of the more obvious gifts from God. Check out VerusGlobal.com to discover ways to elevate organizations to new heights through culture-building leadership trainings:

www.VerusGlobal.com

Dr. Roger Teel, senior minister and spiritual director at Denver's Mile Hi Church in Lakewood, Colorado—thank you for modeling that extraordinary combination of extraordinary heart, leading-edge wisdom and God-centered caring. Oh the lives you and your teams touch! See:

www.MileHiChurch.org.

Drs. Ron and May Hulnick and the University of Santa Monica, the way you've made soul-centered psychology relevant, effective and downright FUN, is art of the highest form. Participating at USM has been by far, my most valuable formal education experience. See:

www.UniversityofSantaMonica.edu .

Werner Erhard, est and the Landmark Forum, thank you for waking me up when I was in my late 20's. Through you I discovered the possibility I might possibly have something to do with how my own life turns out. You taught me personal responsibility and helped launch me in the expression of my life purpose. Wow! See:

www.LandmarkWorldwide.com .

Donna Svendsen, Katie Peterson, Kimberly Martin, all the Champion Team Leaders, LCA Consultants, participants of the Love, Courage and Achievement Project, and all of my individual consulting clients; thank you for your in-the-trenches training. Thank you for trusting me, for the courage to be vulnerable and for tenaciously using the tools to better your lives. Thank you especially for the accelerating impact you make in the world. You have given me the indescribably delicious treat of dancing to the music of your journey. Thank you!

Mark Gelotte, you are a soul-centered artist and book designer. Working with you continues to be an absolute pleasure.

Cara Cantarella and Laura High, thank you for your seasoned competence and soul-centered editing.

Dear God, thank You so much for this gift of life. Thank you for the miracle of allowing me to live in authentic, meaningful, ongoing relationship with You. Thank you for loving me.

About the Author and the
LOVE, COURAGE AND ACHIEVEMENT PROJECT

I was born in Phoenix, Arizona and raised in Scottsdale. After graduating from Arizona State University, I moved to Denver, Colorado, to manifest what I knew to be my destiny; commercial real estate investing. In 1981, I fell in love with Amy and married this brilliant lady in December of that year.

In 1983, my daughter Heather was born. That was the best day of my life. What a miracle she has turned out to be.

A few years later, I experienced the first real dark night of my soul. I was asleep to what really mattered and didn't know it. I alienated my wife, went through bankruptcy and divorce. I lost my family, my home, my reputation, my confidence and my possessions.

Interestingly enough, my brother Bill was going through a similar experience. When we got to the other side, we had both been mightily humbled. From this humility, we began to awaken to a higher possibility of living.

As a divorce attorney, Bill began sharing uncommon insights with clients. Inspired by their breakthroughs, he began to lead small workshops. Bill wrote a book, entitled, "How to Heal a Painful Relationship," which was featured on Oprah.

One day, walking along a railroad track in Galveston, Texas— Bill suggested I, too, could lead seminars for a living. Following his counsel was one of the best decisions I've ever made.

Bill gave up his law practice. I gave up my real estate career and neither of us have regretted those decisions. The de facto partnership we've enjoyed for over three decades has been precious to me beyond description.

In 1998, I graduated from the University of Santa Monica with a Master's degree in Spiritual Psychology. The emphasis of this astounding program is heart-centered counseling. That same year, I began facilitating culture-building leadership trainings for Pathways to Leadership (later named Verus Global). For six years, I had the privilege of teaching corporate leaders in Mexico, Spain, Germany, Thailand and extensively throughout the United States.

Two more marriages and divorces delivered gut-wrenching lessons that ultimately blasted my heart open even more, taught me volumes and drew me even closer to God.

It's taken decades to discover that my highest path was never to become the zillionaire I originally set out to be. Instead, my path has been to fall head over heels in love with my Maker, discovering a dimension of living that I never knew existed.

In my passion to share this higher possibility of life, I founded the Love, Courage and Achievement Project, a Colorado-based organization, dedicated to personal and organizational transformation. Through television, seminars, individual consulting and speaking engagements—participants and work teams grow up the Wisdom Curve, becoming more joyful and effective in their lives.

For more information on the LCA Project, go to:

www.LCAProject.com/shop

For information on scheduling me as a speaker, go to:

www.RandyFerguson.com

If you know someone who might benefit from reading this book, or to enjoy some of our other resources, please go to:

www.lcaproject.com/shop

Made in the USA
Monee, IL
06 November 2019